Turtle
on a
Fencepost

Little Lessons of
Large Importance

A Turtle on a Fencepost

Allan C. Emery
Introduction by Billy Graham

WORD BOOKS
PUBLISHER
4800 WEST WACO DRIVE
WACO, TEXAS
76703

A Turtle on a Fencepost

All Scripture quotations, unless otherwise noted, are from the King James or Authorized Version of the Bible.

ISBN 0–8499–2869–9

Library of Congress Catalog Card Number: 79–63946

Printed in the United States of America

The account concerning Benedict Arnold quoted on page 89 is taken from *MY STORY:* Being the Memoirs of Benedict Arnold: Late Major General in the Continental Army and Brigadier-General in that of His Britannic Majesty—by F. J. Stimson, p. 622. Published by Charles Scribner's Sons, New York.

Contents

Introduction

A Turtle on a Fencepost is one of the most unique books I have ever read. You will not be able to put it down. I am delighted that it has been written. I encouraged my longtime friend Allan Emery, who is now president of the Billy Graham Evangelistic Association (among many other responsibilities), to write it. It is amusing—warm—practical—biblical—and challenging.

This is no surprise to me, because those are all terms which describe its author. His warmth and humor are evident to all who meet him. His intensely practical nature—stemming in part from an outstanding business career—has given him a concern for the practical application of the gospel to every area of life. But most of all, Allan Emery is a man who is rooted in the Scriptures and demonstrates it in his life. His dedication to Christ and his kingdom has been an inspiration to me across the years—as it has been to countless others as well.

This book is written out of a lifetime of experience and study. Allan Emery grew up in a home where Christ was honored. His father was an outstanding Christian layman. That tradition of Christian service was passed to Allan—who in turn has passed it on to his own family. He stands as a living example of what can happen when Christ is exalted in a family from one generation to the next. Allan Emery also served admirably as an officer in the United States Coast Guard during World War II. He had some of the most unusual experiences in that great war of anyone with whom I have talked.

More than anything else, Allan Emery is convinced that Jesus Christ is concerned with every area of our lives, every hour of the day. This is a truth he has demonstrated in his own life—in his family, his business, his service on numerous boards, and his personal witness. It is also a truth we need to hear today. Many people have been especially blessed by the Bible studies he has held in his home for many years. My prayer is that many more people will be blessed by this delightful book. I certainly have been, and I believe every reader will be also.

BILLY GRAHAM

Preface

Thirty-one years ago Marian and I were led of the Lord to start a Bible Club for high school young people in our home. We have never placed a phone call nor sent a postcard to invite them to come. They are invited by classmates and friends. Over the years many have found meaning and direction in life in the Lord Jesus. Scores now serve him in the ministry and on the mission field. During these years I have used illustrations from life to present moral principles. I have been encouraged by clubbers and friends to preserve a few of these experiences in book form. That is the purpose of this book. It is our desire that these life experiences may be a blessing to you and to those to whom you minister. It is only because we know God still uses "loaves and fishes" placed in his hand that we presume to offer this in his name.

A
Turtle
on a
Fencepost

A. Thurber

A Turtle on a Fencepost

Boston's Logan Airport is not the crossroads of the world, but it often seems to be the crossroads of my life, meeting planes, taking visitors to their flights, and boarding or disembarking myself every week. It is always exciting for me to watch the final approach of aircraft and hear the thunder of departing jets. The people represent a cross section of life. I have discovered no better entertainment than watching the reunions at the arrival gates. There is joy and shared sorrow, disappointment and hilarity. At times I have to meet private jets. On these occasions I am led by a station wagon with a flashing yellow roof light down the taxi lanes to the tarmac where the jet will be parked. I am a child again and relish the routine. What means most, however, is the opportunity of conversation with men and women whom I otherwise would see only in board meetings and never really get to know.

One morning I picked up Dr. Robert Lamont to drive him to a meeting. He was flying in from Pittsburgh where he at that time was pastor of the First Presbyterian Church. In the relaxed drive to Hamilton he spoke of his work in such a way that I felt he viewed himself as a spectator to what God had done through his ministry. I suggested that much of what had been accomplished must be because of his gifts and talents. He replied, "Allan, when I was a schoolboy we would occasionally see a turtle on a fencepost and when we did, we knew someone had put him there. He didn't get there by himself. That is how I see my own life. I'm a turtle on a fencepost."

How often I have thought of this imagery! The Bible is replete with examples of men and women who saw themselves as turtles on a fencepost. They knew that their positions of influence and authority were given them by God for his service. They had not arrived by themselves.

Joseph must have thought back over the years of hardship as he watched his brothers bow before him. Beloved of his father and hated by his brothers, Joseph had been sold into slavery in Egypt. As overseer in the house of Potiphar he had resisted the enticement of his master's wife. Being falsely accused, he was thrown into prison. Years later he was brought into the Pharaoh's presence to interpret a dream, and was made ruler of the great empire of Egypt under Pharaoh. After Jacob's death the brothers of Joseph were afraid of revenge and asked for mercy and forgiveness. Joseph responded, "But as for you, ye thought evil against me; but God meant it unto good" (Gen. 50:20). Joseph recognized the sovereignty of God in his life. He saw himself as the means God used in saving his family and building a people. It was all of God and to God belonged the glory.

Moses responded to the command of God to lead the children of Israel out of slavery with the words, "Who am I, that I should go unto Pharaoh and that I should bring forth the children of Israel out of Egypt?" (Exod. 3:11).

Gideon's response to the angel of the Lord's direction to lead an army against the occupying army of the Midianites was, ". . . behold, my family is poor in Manasseh, and I am the least in my father's house" (Judg. 6:15).

Throughout his life David retained a sense of humility and his psalms show us his dependence upon the Lord. But David had to be reminded by the Lord, "I took thee from the sheepcote, from following the sheep, to be ruler over my people, over Israel" (2 Sam. 7:8).

Isaiah saw his sin against the glory and righteousness of God and said "Woe is me! for I am undone; because I am a man of unclean lips, and I dwell in the midst of a people of unclean lips; for mine eyes have seen the King, the LORD of hosts" (Isa. 6:5). While he recognized his inadequacy, he knew the Lord's sufficiency and his answer to the Lord's commission was, "Here am I; send me" (Isa. 6:8).

Jeremiah was confronted with the task of warning his people of judgment for their idolatry and remonstrated, "Then said I, oh, Lord God! behold, I cannot speak; for I am a child" (Jer. 1:6). God touched his mouth and Jeremiah went out in God's power to be his faithful servant even in prison and in the miry pit (Jer. 38:6).

Mary referred to her low estate and the high honor she was to be given. As events occurred in the life of her son, Jesus, she continued to "ponder them in her heart" (Luke 2:19).

The apostle Paul viewed himself progressively as unworthy of the grace that had been given him. In 1 Corinthians 15:9 he refers to himself as "the least of the apostles." In Ephesians 3:8 he calls himself "the least of all saints." And in 1 Timothy 1:15 he sees himself as the chief of sinners. In the objective view of his own inadequacy he is persuaded of the power of God to accomplish through him God's eternal purposes. In Philippians 4:13 he exclaims: "I can do all things through Christ which strengtheneth me." Paul could view his position in life and his life ministry as being a "turtle on a fencepost." He hadn't done it in himself. Someone had put him there.

As I meet men of position and accomplishment I see them view their successes with humility and appear detached from the honors presented them. The greater the men, the more this is so.

I remember attending a meeting in the Grand Ballroom

of the Waldorf Astoria many years ago. Billy Graham was to be presented with the Salvation Army's "Man of the Year Award." I was sitting at a table way to the rear in the balcony. There was the noise of conversation and waiters clearing tables. I thought of those who had recently received this honor—Gen. Douglas MacArthur, Gen. Dwight D. Eisenhower, and other prominent names in service to the nation. Those sitting about me appeared more curious than interested in the acceptance remarks of Mr. Graham.

The presentation was made and Mr. Graham replied, "There are many here who deserve this honor more than I. I accept this award as I accept every honor, temporarily, as one day I shall lay it at the feet of Jesus Christ."* Those around me were transfixed. Cigars went dead and total silence reigned throughout the vast banquet hall. And then Mr. Graham presented the reasons why he knew he would see Jesus, not because of anything good he had done, but because of what the Lord Jesus Christ had done on the cross. Again I saw one who viewed himself as just a "turtle on a fencepost." Someone had put him there.

* Paraphrased as I remember it.

Jesus Loves Me, This I Know

Every evening, after dinner, our family and guests would gather in the living room to have a "sing." We never missed this devotional time. There were occasions when I should have liked to have escaped, but attendance was not optional—it was inevitable and as unavoidable as sunrise. It was one of the routine events in life to be enjoyed, endured, or suffered through. The attitude depended upon my priorities at the time.

Generally this was a happy time and a unifying experience. The devotional began with singing. Mother played the piano beautifully, and with emotional effect. Today in memory I can hear hymns as she played them, just as surely as if I were back in those childhood days. Daddy led the service and picked the hymns or gave us our choices. We sang five or six songs, and then daddy read from the Scripture. Often he commented upon the reading and prayed. We all, guests included, went to our knees and we closed with the Lord's Prayer.

The devotions were always more emotional when grandpa (mother's father) was there, as he became quite moved by the singing. His favorite hymn was "Shall We Gather at the River?" He might comment upon the appropriateness of the words, "Soon we'll reach the shining river, soon our pilgrimage will cease," as they pertained to his own pilgrimage. He was certainly prepared for this event, but the prospect of leaving us all touched him and communicated a touch of sadness to the triumph of the song.

In later years when mother's varicose ulcer made playing difficult, my sister Elsie would play the piano. The family had good voices, but daddy's voice drowned out all the others, so the effect was that of a solo with strong support from the choir.

I learned a great deal from the Scriptures during our family altar, but the strongest impression was the priority of this worship service in my parents' lives. If we were on a ship sailing to California or to Europe, we always had our "reading." If we were enroute to Florida or Arizona, we had our "reading." If we were in the woods of Canada, we had our "reading" and the guide was invited to attend.

In addition to this formal time, both my parents would read Bible stories or tell them (which to a child seemed more exciting). There were other books, too—*Robin Hood,* most of Dickens, Louisa May Alcott, Mark Twain, poetry, the Elsie Dinsmore Series, *Youth's Companion, Robinson Crusoe, Swiss Family Robinson, Gulliver's Travels, Black Beauty, Uncle Tom's Cabin, Billy Whiskers, The Count of Monte Cristo,* and many other works of Dumas. In later life, when I read Dumas on my own, I was amazed at how censored the tales had been when read by mother. Mother told wonderful stories, too. There was the series about Felicia, the white monkey, stories about animals, and bad boys and very good boys. All stories had a moral that we could quickly understand. Beyond all stories was a quality of life that conveyed indelible impressions upon us children. I'll share one illustration.

I must have been six at the time, as I had just received a tricycle, or a velocipede as they were called in those days. My waking hours were lived on this vehicle. We had a tarred drive and a circle by the house that provided ideal cruising conditions. When I awakened one morning a north-easter was in progress. The wind was coming in off the ocean, and the rain was driving against the windows. I was imprisoned. My great source of joy was gone. Feeling betrayed, abused and undone, I entered mother's room looking like a thundercloud. I was letting the world know of my frustration and bitterness—perhaps even at mother, for not having better control over the weather. She instantly appraised my needs and said, "Hello, little boy, what is your name? My, you look unhappy, and on such a day as this when the flowers and trees and grass that have been so thirsty are getting such a good drink." There was a pause for my reply, but none came. I was deep in self-pity and keenly feeling the injustice of life.

Mother went on. "You know, I have a boy who looks like you. He has blond hair and a lovely smile, and if he were here he'd make you the most beautiful castles out of the blocks under my bed. Sometimes he makes tunnels for his train to go through. This is a perfect day for making castles. Why don't you go out and see if you can find him? His name is Allan and he is so smart at building things. See if you can find him." Then she called, "Allan, Allan, there is a friend here who wants to find you."

I disappeared—and when I returned there was, I'm sure, an embarrassed smile on my face. As I appeared, transformed in visage and attitude, mother said, "Allan, where have you been? While you were away a little boy came by who was so unhappy. I guess he didn't realize how good God is to give us rainy days." While she was still speaking I was busily unpacking my blocks to create the most beautiful castle yet, and I knew when it was completed mother would tell an exciting story about it—in which *I* would be the hero in rescuing the beautiful princess held captive by her wicked uncle in its highest tower. Mother and daddy always seemed to see the best in us and determined to develop our own appreciation of ourselves and the gifts God gave us.

I rather suspect that my first understanding of the cross and its meaning came while sitting in mother's lap as she showed me a picture of the crucifixion in color printed in a linen book. She said, "Allan, Jesus died for your sins, just as he died for mine, and we have to accept his dying for us as his loving present to us. Each night as we ask God to forgive us for all the naughty things we have done, we can know that God does forgive us because Jesus took the blame for our badness upon himself. Do you understand?"

I told her I did. It seemed very sad that someone so good would have to die for someone so bad as I, but I did understand. This didn't prevent me from fighting at school, teasing, lying at convenient times, indulging in self-interest and pure selfishness. I guess I believed that if the world were not created entirely for my enjoyment, the creation must have been engineered with my happiness largely in mind.

With the theology of 1 John 1:9 firmly settled in my young mind, I felt relatively safe in my hedonistic, self-centered activities. There were unending adventures. These involved sleeping outdoors in a tent and watching the horses being shod by the blacksmith. The smell of the red hot shoe being placed on the horse's hoof is a never-to-be-forgotten odor. There was haying and the trampling down of the hay in the barn, fruit gathering all through the summer with varieties of apples, pears, plums, cherries, and peaches. There were chores like picking blueberries, beans, peas—and picking rosebugs off the roses. For the latter I received the best pay, five cents per hundred! Daddy would count the carcasses upon his return at night.

Dandelion digging in the lawn was endless, and held little job satisfaction. But—riding in the rumble seat was an opportunity to be an airplane pilot and I wore my goggles—feeling very professional. My greater sins involved snowball fights, and in snowless months fighting with horse buns, tomatoes or rotten apples. When we gave up raising chickens, the chicken coop became my clubhouse. I had a tree house, and several dens in the woods. I sailed boats in a spring, and on rainy days in the bathtub. We had great naval battles and, at times, used only sail upon which we blew until exhausted. We explored the cubbyholes on the third floor, and were able to travel from one end of the house to the other, appearing in any room we chose. We climbed trees, tried sheets for parachutes—with disastrous results, we rode bicycles, carts, hand-cars and scooters. There was never a halt in our activity.

Our parents used parables or illustrations for teaching. If I didn't come immediately upon being called, mother told the story of the little boy whose mother saw a snake behind him. When called by his mother he said, "In a minute." By that time the snake had bitten the boy.

One of the most vivid stories was about Charlie. Charlie was a pretty good boy, but he told lies so often he didn't even know he was telling them. His parents tried to discipline him by spanking him and even sending him to his room without supper. Nothing worked. Charlie kept on lying. Finally, his father said, "Charlie, every time you tell a lie I am going to put a nail in the barn door."

Charlie thought this was a great idea, because it wouldn't hurt like spanking. One nail didn't look bad sticking out from the barn door, but in a short time there were dozens, and these attracted the attention of the farmhands, visitors, relatives, and even the pastor. Soberly Charlie's daddy would explain what these nails stood for—Charlie's lies.

After the nails had accumulated for a month, Charlie said, "Daddy, I'm never going to tell a lie again. Will you take the nails out?" His father replied that he would take out all the nails when Charlie had gone a whole month without telling a lie. Charlie counted the days and on the thirty-first morning he raced to his dad shouting, "Today is the day you promised to take out the nails." With hammer in hand Charlie's father went with him to the barn and pulled out every nail. When the last nail had been extracted Charlie stepped back to see the results, and then burst into tears. His father asked him why he was crying. When Charlie was able to speak, he said between sobs, "The nails are gone but the marks are still there." This story was to explain

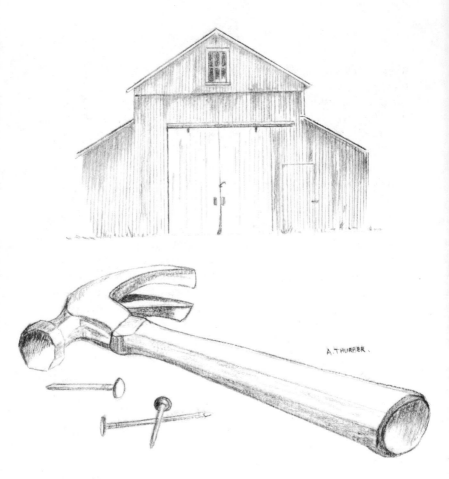

that while God's forgiveness in Christ is complete, the results and consequences of sin remain upon our lives.

Example was our greatest teacher. My parents never "taught" the importance of Bible reading and prayer. They just practiced it. In the morning daddy used the "Yellow Room" for devotions. I was always an early riser, and every time I passed this room I'd hear daddy praying. He prayed out loud so his mind would not wander. Guests and new help might pass this door thinking there was someone with daddy, and we children knew there was. We'd hear our own names mentioned and we knew his greatest desire in life was for us to grow up to be Christian men and women.

Our church was "gathered" in 1623 and was known as The Old North Church of Weymouth. William Smith, the father of Abigail Smith Adams, was the pastor of this church for many years. The manse where Abigail was born in 1744 and where she was married to John Adams in 1764, still stands. My great-great-uncle Joshua Emery was pastor of the church from 1830 to 1865, and during this period founded two daughter churches—Pilgrim Congregational Church in North Weymouth and the Union Congregational Church in East Braintree. We can see the steeple from our house and I could run to Sunday school in four minutes.

I can't say that church was an exciting and rich experience. There were no nurseries or youth programs in my early years, so I had to sit in the straight-backed, enclosed pews with the red cushions on Sunday morning. I could lie down without being seen. Mother provided picture books for me, much to the envy of my less-indulged friends. They would vie with each other to be my guest. A few times I escaped confinement by crawling under the pews. Once away, there was little that my parents could do to impede my progress without disrupting the service. My advance could be clearly detected by the reactions of the parishioners in the pews ahead. Daddy would be very upset after the service and mother would scold me, and break up laughing doing so.

The sermons were dull and wholly beyond me, I'm sure, even had I listened. The deacons wore cutaways. The choir sang from the loft, and the organ was pumped by a volunteer who ran the affair by vigorously moving a pump handle up and down. The speed required depended upon the volume the organist was using. One time the "Doxology" was due to be sung. The first powerful strains of the introduction died out, and there was some commotion as the organist had to awaken the pumper, who had dozed off. Events like this made church endurable.

In my early years I used to insist on sitting in mother's lap so as to see over the high siding of the pew. This worked out in winter, when I wore knickers, but when I wore short

pants the beads on mother's dress were very uncomfortable.
I remember the entertaining experience of standing on the
cushion and watching those behind and to the side of our
pew sing the hymns. One man had an enormous Adam's
apple that performed all sorts of gyrations when he sang.
I tried to touch it but he never cooperated and mother
discouraged my curiosity. I became able to distinguish each
voice and found that people became distracted by being
stared at.

At times I'd embarrass mother by asking her why Mr.
_____ had no chin, and why Mr. _____ had such a
big nose, and why Mrs. _____ always sang the same note.
Also, there was the problem of my dime for the offering;
I always dropped it on the floor, where it sometimes rolled
on its edge into another pew. As I review my early exposure
to church, I can believe these days took their toll upon
my parents as well. I had the feeling I was well, if not
favorably known in the church and learned later that all
prophecy concurred in predicting my being the black sheep
of the family, if not the first member of the family in many
generations to be hanged. At this point, I'll have to state
that our three children were positive angels compared to
me. My wife Marian's genes are credited with the improve-
ment.

Compared to church, Sunday school was fun. We had
an orchestra which to me was a symphony. We also had
to memorize a great deal of Scripture, for which I am grateful
to this day. Daddy taught a junior high class; the course
was on the Book of Proverbs; the first required memory
verse was Proverbs 1:10, "My son, if sinners entice thee,
consent thou not." Daddy's personal illustrations made this
course extremely popular. I can still see him, dressed in
his striped trousers and swallowtail coat, teaching with one
foot on the seat, facing two or three pews of boys. Church
and Sunday school were important to me because they were
so to him.

At the age of twelve I joined the church, after attending
the Pastor's Preparation Class. All the kids joined at twelve,

and no one flunked the course. The chief benefit, as I remember, was being able then to take communion and the gift of a radio and electric alarm clock for the occasion. At ten I had received a Bible, and this was a most significant gift. From that time onward I never missed reading at least a chapter a day. In later years during the war I was able to recite a chapter instead of reading one when in total darkness at my battle station.

In those days I slept in the room directly beneath the cupola. In the winter it was bitterly cold there, but I liked hearing the wind rattle the windows and it was an adventure. I had my radio, and when I went to bed at eight, I was allowed to listen to my radio until eight-thirty. Sunday nights I listened to Tremont Temple Baptist Church, where Dr. J. Whitcomb Brougher was the pastor. He told the best stories and funniest jokes. One night he spoke from John 3, and he explained, to my understanding, that salvation was a personal relationship between the Lord Jesus Christ and the believer. One could not be saved by being good, nor by one's church membership, nor by family respectability or position. One must be "born again."

The Holy Spirit made this truth very real to me. When Dr. Brougher asked for a decision, I slipped onto the cold floor and said, "Dear God, You know I'm not very good. I know I've sinned and I really don't have much to offer You. I'm not the best student in the class; I'm not the best runner on the track team; I'm not the most popular kid in school by far. I have only $361.00 in the North Weymouth Cooperative Bank, but You can have me now and for the rest of my life. I want to exchange my badness for Your goodness. I want to be of use to You and I accept Your promise to make me 'born again' through your Son, Jesus."

I climbed back into bed and never from that day to this have I feared death. Earlier I had worried that the rest of the family might be in heaven and I'd be left. Now I knew that I shared the greatest promise of life. I was a child of God in a personal way. I had submitted to his claims upon my life—and the reality of the Cross, Resurrection and Second Coming were sealed to me. From that moment to this, I have been wholly convinced that a transaction took place that transcends time and eternity. The Love I had understood as a child depicted on an awful Roman cross had been made available for me. As I had been the beloved child of wonderful parents, I was now the child of a King. The song I had sung so lustily in our "readings" was indeed a fact—*Jesus Loves Me, This I Know.*

A. THURBER

What Would Daddy Do?

Today I find myself still asking myself, "What would daddy do?" when confronted with those decisions in business and in life that are so often not black and white, but gray. I am in debt to the memory-making efforts that my father made to imprint indelibly upon my mind the meaning of "integrity." The word "integrity" comes from the Latin *integritas* meaning "whole." Unlike many English words, it has maintained its meaning for centuries. In its sense of "wholeness" Sir Thomas More wrote, "To the integrity whereof (Christ's body) the blood of the same pertaineth." Dr. Johnson used the word in its sense of rectitude, virtue, and honesty: "I promised that when I possessed the power, I would use it with inflexible integrity." Integrity is an element of character we long to see in business, political, and academic leadership. We see the pressure of the expedient to bend decisions and policies. Compromise replaces integrity. I want to share some examples of what I saw in my father's life to give meaning to this word for me.

One day I was handing up wool fleeces to my father and a customer in the loft above our offices on Summer Street in Boston. We had sample bags of large lots in our loft. These represented the wool stored in other parts of

Boston and the country. The buyer had examined a number of lots when he told my father he would buy them and then he said, "Mr. Emery, in the future I will only look at wool in _ ____ warehouse as I share ownership in that warehouse." As the buyer was an employee of his company, daddy knew the buyer was using his position for personal benefit. Dad replied, "We use that warehouse, but I don't believe we can show wool to you there in the future." The buyer understood, and we never sold him a pound of wool thereafter. I asked my father why we couldn't store wool in this buyer's warehouse, since the cost would be the same. He replied, "We would be encouraging him in the use of his power of purchasing for a conflict of interest against his employer."

Before the turn of the century, when my father went to West Texas to buy wool, the center of wool buying was San Angelo. There were dozens of saloons and the business between grower and wool buyer was usually transacted there. Daddy was told that to buy wool he would have to buy drinks for the grower, and that the day when most ranchers were in town was Sunday. He replied, "I'll never buy a drink for anyone, and I'll never buy wool on Sunday." They laughed at him and he responded, "I'll buy more than anyone and I'll do it my way." He did that. Some years we bought over half the weight of Texas wool produced. Our buyers were never allowed to work on the Lord's Day. There was never any question that this was company policy.

Whenever we took the train to Boston and the conductor missed taking our ticket, we would always have to find the conductor or ticket collector and present our ticket to him. Regardless of time pressure, we surrendered the tickets.

My grandfather, Edward Conant, lost his father when he was very young. He and his mother eked out a scant living. He helped by selling newspapers and later went into the hardware business as an apprentice. Ultimately he became a proprietor of the store. With his savings from this business he started an investment business, using his own capital and that of friends and relatives. His investments were successful until he invested in apple orchards in Kansas. Before the trees ever bore fruit, grasshoppers destroyed the trees and the loss to investors was total. It took my grandfather eleven years to pay back the loss to those who trusted his judgment. Although he had no legal liability, he felt a moral obligation. God honored him and he was a great blessing to many.

Integrity is doing what is right in spite of the cost—even when no one is looking!

One day while I was a sample clerk my father received a call from an old and reliable customer. The customer said that a large delivery of Texas "twelve-months" wool contained needlegrass in the bellies. We knew the customer could not produce his quality cloth with this vegetable defect. My father replied that he had told the salesman to be certain to call attention to this fault, but that was the only wool of his staple and quality available. The customer replied, "Maybe he did tell me, but I don't remember it." My father replied, "If you don't remember being told, it is our fault and we will make it good. Sort out the bellies and we will pay for the labor and replace the lost weight with other wool." I was getting $10 a week then, and I asked my father what that would cost. "About $20,000 before we are through." There was no thought of loss. If we made a mistake, we would pay for it. I asked, "Didn't the salesman tell him?" "I'm certain he did," daddy assured, "but if he didn't leave the customer with the memory of it, he failed and, as our agent, we are responsible for his failure."

Insurance was another area where daddy was meticulous to see that our claims were wholly justified. Once he lost a pair of fine German binoculars. He collected insurance only to find the binoculars a year later. Immediately he sent a check to the company and received a letter back stating that this seldom occurred and that they were encouraged. It was a small thing, but children never forget examples lived before them.

One morning we shopped at a small fruit store in

Lyndhurst, on the west coast of England. A lad, obviously poor, handed the store owner a shilling to purchase some beautiful yellow bananas on the counter. The proprietor drew from under the counter some overripe bananas and handed them to the boy. The boy asked for his shilling back but the proprietor said, "They're good enough for the likes of you." At such times daddy reacted with the speed of lightning. He told the man to give the boy what he had bought. Daddy was told to mind his own business, to which he replied, "You give the boy those bananas or I'll report you to the Bobby outside." The lad got his good yellow bananas. I was young myself then, but I learned that integrity demands becoming involved with justice for others.

Most people want to be fair and honest. Sometimes we have to help them along. It is important to separate principle from personality. As I write, I sit in a plane enroute to Boston. It is another of those eighteen-hour working days that seem like a week. The problem in which I was involved today required my straightforwardly telling a customer that what he intended to do was contrary to his trusteeship; that he was submitting to political influences totally at variance to what I knew to be his life reputation. He was shaken. I do not know what his final decision will be, but I felt perfectly confident in saying lovingly what was necessary— because I could hear my father saying it himself.

One day a teenager rang the doorbell, and as Marian opened the door, she saw one of our Bible Club girls in tears. As the girl sat down on the living room couch, the flood-gates opened and it was a while before she could speak. When she did stop crying she told this story: Her mother had demanded that she tell the neighbors her mother's new coat had been purchased at Filene's and not at the Bargain Center. The mother had even sewn a Filene's label into the coat. The daughter kept saying, "It would be a lie and she told me I must tell a lie."

How often we hear a parent say, "Tell her I'm not home," when a child answers the phone. What does this do to a child? Children understand principles. They find security in rules and standards. Parents are on display daily before their children. Children have more time to observe them than parents have to observe the children. Children will accept error in judgment on the part of their parents, but wrong motivation and hypocrisy will destroy respect and trust. A parent has the greatest opportunity for creating Christian character of all influences in a child's life. I believe the greatest tribute a child can pay to a parent is to face the decisions of life with the confident answer to the question, "What would daddy or mother do?"

I was sitting in the shade of a lovely patio overlooking the ocean when I asked a question I had long wanted to ask Tom Sykes. When we had chosen a representative to purchase wool for us, we had chosen Tom because of his reputation for total honesty. Tom would deliver wool equal to or better than type every time—even on a fast-rising market when he may have sold short. So I asked, "Tom, why are you so scrupulously honest?" He replied, "My grandfather spent time with me. He made me realize that I was important to him and that how I lived my life mattered tremendously. Grandfather told stories and gave illustrations that I still remember, and often he would close with these words, 'You can sell your honor for eighteen pence, but you can't buy it back.' There have been times when I have been tempted to take 'short cuts' but I have heard ringing in my ears this expression used by my grandfather and my father, and I see clearly where duty lies." I realized that Tom was telling me that he, too, still asked, "What would daddy do?"

Tools or Idols

It was an early May morning when my father, his driver, his captain, and I drove across the Sagamore Bridge crossing the Cape Cod Canal. The ribbon of blue beneath us curved between the sandy cliffs, and to the east was Cape Cod Bay and farther to the west Buzzards Bay. I wonder if I was ever more excited. The year was 1935, and I was to receive a long-awaited present for my sixteenth birthday.

In our family sixteen was a special age, and a special present was given to each of us five children upon reaching this milestone. I knew my present was to be a sailing boat. I had a small sailboat for some time, but this would be a large one. Daddy had brought his captain along. This man handled and cared for the "commuter" that he used to go to work each good summer day. While in Boston he would travel by boat to the different wool warehouses about the harbor, where he examined purchases or showed wool to prospective buyers. We were going to sail the new boat home and spend the night on her, so it should be a big boat. I didn't think I could bear the suspense. What if she were ugly or a poor sailer? Could I hide my disappointment? Daddy wore the satisfied expression of having a good surprise. I supposed I could relax a little.

We stopped at the boat yard at Osterville and unloaded the car—bags, charts, jackets, and food. A dozen or more boats lay moored in the tight little harbor, and at the pier lay a yawl, a Crosby cat, and an Alden Malabar sloop.

We were met by a gentleman wearing a battered yachting cap and white trousers spotted by recent painting activities. He pointed to the Alden sloop. It was black with white trim, shined brass, gleaming mahogany brightwork, and teak decks. The mast shot up fifty feet. Daddy said, "Allan, the black one is your birthday present."

I had never seen anything made by man more beautiful. With her perfect shear and balance, she looked at peace with herself and the element for which she was designed. A great wave of pride swept over me, and in rapid succession I imagined myself sailing into our home port, the admiration of my friends, the envy of some rivals. I dreamed of exploring the New England coast, and entering the Bermuda Race or even the Halifax Race. I felt the pride of ownership, and of command, and of adventure.

In those few seconds I heard my father continue, "Your mother and I are happy to give this to you, as we know you will use it as a tool to lead your Sunday school boys to Jesus Christ." I was stunned! That was not what I had been thinking about.

We went aboard the sloop. The dependable engine, the neat galley, the snug bunks, and the comfortable eating area were great, but it was not until we hoisted sail and headed out into Nantucket Sound that I realized what a beautiful ship the *Martin Pring* truly was. As long as we sailed her, she served well, not just in providing enjoyment, developing skills, and bringing us through gales and fogs safely, but also in being the *tool* daddy had bought her for. I never sailed in the Bermuda Race nor in the Halifax Race, but each weekend, or on longer trips along the Maine coast and the Elizabeth Islands, the *Martin Pring* was the means of presenting the claims of Jesus Christ to young lads.

My parents consistently taught us that all we had must be held in an open hand, that when we closed our fingers tightly over anything placed in our trust, we lost the joy and the blessing. Things acquired as an end in themselves became idols and possessed us. We became slaves to anything not willingly given or shared. The enemy tries to make us part of the world system of values. In 1 John 2:15–17 we learn that the world's values are not the Christian's; verse 16 tells us:

> For all that is in the world—
> the lust of the flesh   (the desire to indulge)
> the lust of the eyes   (the desire to acquire)
> the pride of life   (the desire to impress)
> is not of the Father, but is of the world.

Our only basis for ownership is to be able to use things as tools—whether they be clothes, cars, boats, or swimming pools. Our family does not have a swimming pool. It is not because we do not swim, nor that we think it extravagant. The reason is simply at our age we do not see a way in which we could justify the expense for its use as a tool. We have friends who use their pool for the congregating of young people in the neighborhood; they have music about the pool in the evening; there is general singing, then some hymns, a Bible study, and the young Christians give testimonies. I believe that this pool has been the means of reaching more youngsters with the gospel than all the youth programs in all the churches in town combined. That pool is a tool.

What kind of a car would Jesus drive if he were here in the flesh today? I do not know, but I do believe he will let us know the kind of car we should drive. It depends upon our individual ministry. I know youth leaders who feel a snappy sport car provides the platform for conversation when working with high school lads. One couple have a four-wheel-drive recreation vehicle to take kids into the mountains. A salesman needs a car that will be reliable for long distances. A car, too, can be a tool or an idol.

We live in a house much too big for just Marian and me. I enjoy living in this home where I grew up, and sleeping in the same room in which I was born. The only remaining justification for the expense of maintaining a place that is today anachronistic is its use for a weekly Bible Club. We have just completed 29 years of Weymouth Bible Club. Each Thursday night we have from 50 to 125 in attendance. We average about 70. The kids handle the music and I bring the Bible study. From this group we have seen more than 50 go to the mission field or into the ministry. About a third are Roman Catholic, a third run the whole gamut of Protestant groups, and a third come from nonchurch backgrounds. The latter, if asked who Matthew, Mark, Luke, and John were, might reply, "Some musical group?" No one is sent to club. One has to be invited by a member.

Marian and I are beginning to feel we are too old to continue Bible club, but the kids keep coming. We can pack 85 into our living room; an overflow sits on the front hallway staircase. So long as the Lord sends the kids, we need the house for a neutral place where young men and women can find meaning in life because they see the Bible teaches that they are the object of the love of God.

We have a boy or girl live with us from time to time. Hardly an evening passes without a visit or phone call from someone with a problem. Last week we were alerted by a worried mother, "Kathy has run away and she will probably show up at your house. Just call me and I'll pick her up." I replied, "If she comes, don't you think she should stay until she calms down?" The mother agreed.

One night I was getting ready to leave to take the "Federal Express" to Washington. It had been a difficult weekend with all kinds of people interruptions. Sunday afternoon a student at a theological seminary called to see if he could come over to ask a question. He said it would only take ten minutes. Four hours later he left. He went away convinced that the Bible itself was a higher authority than his professors, and with a peace and joy he had experienced when still in club.

I had allocated a half hour to eat supper, a half hour to pack and change clothes, and a half hour to read out loud to Marian. The phone rang. A soft voice on the line was another interruption. Paula said that she and Debbie wanted to talk to Marian and me. I looked at my date book and suggested a Wednesday evening of the next week as the first open time I had. Paula replied, "But we have to see you tonight." I told her about my having to get the sleeper, but I knew we had to see her. I asked if she could get to the house.

Since her parents were away, we drove to Paula's home. There we picked her up and Debbie as well. I admit to impatience—and immediately asked, "What is the problem?" I shall never forget Paula's answer. "Last night I dreamed I died and I knew I wasn't ready to die. I was afraid, for you see, Mr. Emery, I've never been born over again." "And what is your problem, Debbie?" I asked. She replied, "I've never been born over again either." That night in front of our fire both Paula and Debbie found Jesus Christ as Savior and Friend. We drove them home, and I was aware that I would have to skip supper and the luxury of a half hour of fellowship with Marian. As we headed back to our house Marian quietly asked, "Was it worth it?" We both laughed. We realized that time, too, is either a tool or an idol. We thanked God for being able to be a tool for him.

The Lower Lights

The sloop *Martin Pring* tugged at her mooring at the Wessagusset Yacht Club. The tide was at the flood, wind NE fifteen knots, and the harbor chop discouraged smaller craft from venturing forth. This was the day of testing, the climax of planning, and the dawn of years of dreaming. Two fellows and I were to make a maiden voyage "Down East" along the coast of Maine.

Early this morning sister Elsie had driven me up to the Club with all our gear—sea bags and provisions for four weeks at sea. We carried ice, blankets, "church clothes" on hangers, and a great box of assorted cookies that Bertha had baked for the voyage. Elsie rode out in the tender with us to pick up the *Martin Pring* and bring her to the pier for taking on water and gasoline for our auxiliary engine. Sail covers came off, the bilge was pumped, the engine started, the mooring cast off, and we tied up at the outer float. Each article was stowed so that no amount of battering by the sea could turn the article into a missile of destruction. An hour later my sister stood on the float as we headed out.

We made sail as soon as we were beyond the anchorage and began our beat to windward across Hingham Bay and out through the tide-rips of Hull Gut, into President Roads, past Boston Harbor Light, and into the open sea. We lay, close-hauled on the starboard tack to weather Cape Ann. The wind was fresh and cool, almost cold. We heeled over nicely to port. There was an ocean swell with a surface chop of two feet. Never in my life had I been more excited. All my dreams were being fulfilled—I was going to sea as skipper of my own packet! I was sixteen.

Sailing out I had looked astern at our home on King Oak Hill. I knew mother would be watching our sail, and what was to me a high adventure would be to her the ultimate test of releasing the "apron strings." My friends and I would be the object of the continuing prayers of mother and daddy.

I climbed the mast to the spreaders to get the "feel" and see the view. We took turns on the bowsprit as the seas came close to our feet. I tried out my bunk, then rode in the tender being towed astern. I took bearings, identified objects along the distant shore, and kept my position accurately recorded on the chart. Columbus, Magellan, Cabot, and Cook never felt more excitement than we did that day. The sun was bright, the wind fair, and nothing could ever go wrong. Lunch consisted of sandwiches (make your own) in the cockpit. The ginger ale was cold from the ice box. Everything tasted superb. The only frustration was in containing all the beauty and excitement.

Our first major course change was made abeam of Thacher's Light. We watched the sun set over Ipswich Bay and headed for Portland Harbor. The wind hauled to SE. We chose our watches and I took the first one because I knew I couldn't sleep. The binnacle light on the compass was comforting in the darkness. The running lights threw their green and red upon the jib. Down below the other fellows were asleep. There was just the sound of spray, the straining of the lines, the wind in the rigging, and the creaking of the vessel. Above me the stars began to fade and the wind freshened. We picked up speed and the seas were building up. We had no radio, and if we had, there were no weather forecasts to mariners in those days. The watch changed and I slept my two hours.

When I came back on deck the air had thickened and the horizon was greatly reduced. I decided to shorten sail. We came up into the wind and we tucked a reef in the mainsail. It was not easy to shorten sail at night on a slippery deck and a pitching, rolling platform. We lay off and were satisfied with the better performance. To keep from luffing, we had to trim sail. The wind was veering to the east.

I felt the first raindrops and soon it was raining steadily. Great sheets of wetness beat upon our oilskins as we were all on deck now. Visibility had dropped to a hundred yards. I felt the first fear. We were making good speed, but now I had no means of checking our position. Our best hope lay in hearing the fog horns off Cape Elizabeth Light and from Portland Lightship. Our course lay for the lightship but the factors of inaccurate steering, windage, and sea effect could put us miles off course. I realized that the wind would carry the fog horn blasts from Cape Elizabeth along the coast rather than to sea. We should pick up the horn from the lightship and possibly hear the ocean bellbuoy.

Had I known what I soon learned, I should have put to sea rather than make port in such conditions. We could expect greater safety from heavy weather than take a chance with surf and rocks. It appeared to me that protection lay in a harbor. The wind was now thirty-five knots from the NE with light rain and fog. No lights showed. No sound was heard except the crash of the seas and the scream of the wind. The glamor of our departure vanished. Fear gripped me, and I tried not to communicate it.

One lad went below and made cocoa for us in crockery mugs. And then we heard it—Portland Lightship. Sound is so distorted in wind and fog. Were we really making our landfall at the right point? The sound faded out and then suddenly we saw her about two hundred yards to lee-ward of us, her light barely a loom in the fog. We had missed the bellbuoy, but we knew where we were now. We altered course down mid-channel between Ram Island and

Portland Head Light. Confidence returned. The night again was total darkness. And then it happened!

We had heard a fog horn far ahead and had been blowing ours at one minute intervals. Suddenly, a blast—and there above us was the bow of a great freighter. The bow lookout was above us with a look of horror on his face. I slammed the tiller to starboard. We lost our wind. Our mast came within a yard or two of the starboard bow of the ship. We passed down her side, so close we could hear swearing on the bridge. We were shaken to our roots. How did we know other vessels did not lie ahead? I decided to steer along the west side of the main channel to preclude another such encounter. The fog was still heavy, and the wind had dropped some, but seas were fierce. We could hear them roaring against the rocks to windward on Ram Island. Our confidence began to return. Of course, no lights were visible. Portland Head Light was enveloped in fog. It cast not a shadow over us. We kept blowing our horn.

Then came a sharp gleam on our port bow. In its ray we could see towering breakers and spray. A figure held a searchlight. He was standing close to the rocks and shouting through a trumpet. Though we never heard a word, we got the message—we were about to go aground! We steered to the center of the channel. Because of our near collision we had almost foundered. The man on the shore in the early morning darkness was the lighthouse keeper. Awake on this wild night, he had heard our horn and from long experience realized we were in too close. He had left the warmth and security of his cottage on a wild night. He had done what had to be done to save us.

The words of the old hymn became real to us all. And this hymn never fails to remind me of my responsibility to other seamen.

> Brightly beams our Father's mercy
> From His lighthouse evermore;
> But to us He gives the keeping
> Of the lights along the shore.

Trim your feeble lamps, my brother!
Some poor seaman, tempest-tossed,
Trying now to make the harbor,
In the darkness may be lost.

Let the lower lights be burning,
Send the gleam across the wave!
Some poor fainting, struggling seaman
You may rescue, you may save.

Kindness Can Make You Cry

Words often change their connotations from generation to generation. When I was a child, the word "black" for Negro would have been considered by my parents as disrespectful. All references to people of African descent were either "Negro" or "colored." I do not believe there were any Negroes living in our town when I was a lad. There were a number of families living in Hingham, which was next door; these families attended the First Baptist Church and were active in the church and community. My only contact with Negroes was with Pullman porters. At that time, due to prejudice in the country, being a Pullman porter offered as great an opportunity to a Negro as could be expected.

Daddy had great respect for the Pullman Company's ability to select such outstanding men, and he insisted that we learn the porter's name from his name card placed just inside the entrance of each car. We were always to call him "Mr. Eastman" or "Mr. Murray" or whatever we found his name to be. In later years, as a buyer and salesman, I would often spend four nights a week sleeping in pullmans. I never found one of these men who was not professional, capable, honest, and, in many cases, a committed Christian.

Some of my greatest lessons were learned in conversation with them, and I am grateful to my father for creating the climate within which I might listen and learn. I wish I might share dozens of experiences, but two will have to suffice.

In the later years of their lives and before the death of my father my parents would often spend time during midwinter in Arizona. This particular year was January 1937. My sister Elsie was to have a mid-semester break at Wheaton College, and it was arranged that our parents and I take the "New England States" Express to Chicago, transfer to the Santa Fe Terminal, and have Elsie join us aboard the "Chief" to Phoenix. I loved trains and still do. The view from the observation car, the fine food impeccably served in the dining car upon spotless linen, the grapefruit in bowls of ice, and the crisp celery and the olives—I loved them all. But, best of all was sleeping in a lower berth, where I could look out into the night to see flashing red lights at railroad crossings and the activity in the stations where we stopped. It was always an adventure, and the click of the rails and the motion lulled me to sleep.

The first evening on the "Chief" was particularly exciting, as this train had many special features. There was a barber shop, two diners, a club car, an observation car—and elegance. After an excellent dinner I told my parents I'd like to go to bed, and I asked the porter if he would make up my bed. I always enjoyed watching this process, as it seemed magical the way a section could be transformed into a lower and upper berth. As the porter moved about, I noticed a limp. He told me he had had an ingrown toenail. A chiropodist had worked on it the previous day, and it had become infected. Obviously he was in great pain. We talked about other subjects and I went to bed, sleeping soundly until breakfast time. During breakfast daddy commented upon the way the porter appeared to be in pain, and I filled him in on the reason. After our meal, I went back in the observation car, returning to our car a half hour later to see the porter coming out of my parents' drawing room.

A. THURBER

As the porter walked toward me, I saw that he was distressed, and as he passed me, his face appeared to fracture and he broke out crying—great tears cascading down his cheeks onto his white jacket. He went into the men's lounge, sat down upon the leather bench, put his hands over his face, and cried. I was embarrassed to see a grown man cry, but I felt he needed attention. So I sat beside him and waited until he had quieted down some. I was particularly concerned because he had just left my father's accommodations. I asked, "Are you crying because your toe hurts?" He replied, "No, it is because of your daddy." This really concerned me, so I pressed for the story.

Daddy and mother had returned from breakfast and daddy had immediately approached the porter, asking about his toe. Daddy told him that he was not a doctor, but he felt he might be able to help him. The porter was reluctant but, at dad's insistence, he went into the drawing room and exposed a toe, terribly inflamed and swollen. Daddy suggested he lance it, clean it out, and bandage it to relieve the pain and expedite healing. The porter agreed and, as he told me of it, he burst out crying again. I asked, "Did it hurt that much?" He said, "It didn't hurt at all, and it feels fine now."

"Then, why are you crying?"

"Well, while he was dressing my toe, your daddy asked me if I loved the Lord Jesus. I told him my mother did but that I did not believe as she did. Then he told me that Jesus loved me and had died for me. As I saw your daddy carefully bandaging my foot, I saw a love that was Jesus' love and I knew I could believe it. We got down on our knees and we prayed and, now, I know I am important to Jesus and that he loves me."

With that he started crying again, happy and unashamed. When his sobs subsided, he earnestly burst out, "You know, boy, kindness can make you cry." I understood. I also understood that a living illustration like this can never be forgotten and the privilege of seeing such events is a responsibility of life.

Daddy was returning from six weeks of buying wool in Texas. From St. Louis he took the "Wolverine" to Boston. He had established a good relationship with the porter, and they had several talks together about their mutual faith. The train was pulling out from Back Bay Station, and in a few minutes the trip would be over, and daddy would be at the South Station and a block from his Summer Street office. He was, naturally, excited about getting home and was ready to leave the train, when the porter approached him and said, "Mr. Emery, do you suppose I could ask you a question after my passengers leave?" So daddy remained and after the last passenger disembarked, the porter returned with his question.

"There were two boys in my family. My mother worked very hard to teach us all she could and to see that we had the best education available at that time. I was a good student. When I had graduated from high school, I went to work as a railroad waiter and then I got this job. My whole desire was to help my mother and fulfill her wish that I go to college and become a preacher. She wanted her life to count by seeing her son a preacher. Well, I saved my money and while I was doing this, my younger brother went in a different direction. He drank and partied and nearly killed himself by living for the devil. About the time I was accepted for college, my brother was converted. He decided he wanted to preach. He had nothing, so he asked me to provide for his education. I was so happy to see this great change in his life, I agreed and today my brother is a nationally known preacher. You may have heard him on the radio. He has led thousands to Christ. So, you see, I couldn't go into the ministry and I am too old now. Mr. Emery, my question is this: Do you suppose the Lord will give me some credit for the souls my brother led to him?"

That night, at the dinner table, when my father told this story he was so deeply moved he nearly broke down. We knew what his answer would have been and that the biblical principle is expressed in Samuel 30:24, "For as his share is who goes down to the battle, so shall his share be who stays by the baggage; they shall share alike" (RSV).

We Gave Him Our Best!

It was two o'clock in the morning. I looked at the figure lying upon the bed in front of me. Two days' growth of beard stubble was on his face. His heavy breathing was the only sound. The smell of alcohol pervaded the room. The city had quieted down. The lone window of the room looked out upon a narrow alley. Occasionally I could hear a window open and the sound of someone using the window as a toilet. In the distance a siren wailed. I felt tired and sorry for myself.

That evening I had been called by my father to go to a certain street where I would find a well-known leader of the community in a drunken condition. My father suggested I take another employee of our company with me. We were to bring the drunk to a mission to protect him and his reputation. Dad would send a doctor to see the man. The doctor arrived, gave him a shot, and told us to be sure that one of us remained with him through the night as he might injure himself if he went out. My associate and I took two-hour shifts. At six in the morning I received a call from my father telling me he was sending his driver to get us and that our ward would go with us to King Oak Hill. We carried the inebriate to the car between us, and he fell into a deep stupor riding between us in the rear seat. As I thought of this man who held a position of trust and responsibility, I felt extremely hostile toward him. He had betrayed a trust, I felt, and I was upset that he had cost me a night's sleep.

Our guest stirred as we turned up our drive. At the front door were my parents, and mother told me where to bring him. The big guest room had fresh flowers on the dresser and, to my horror, I saw that mother had made up the four-poster bed with real linen hemstitched sheets and linen monogrammed pillow cases. We put our limp burden on the bed and prepared to undress him. I went to mother and told her she knew nothing about drunks, that when he woke up he'd throw up over the bed, sheets, and antique bedspread. She looked at me very seriously and said, "When he wakes up he'll feel sick, lonely, and ashamed. It is important for him to see immediately that he is our honored guest and that we gave him our best." To me it had been "casting pearls before swine." To her it was killing the fatted calf "for this my son who was lost is found."

Recently our Allan III brought home a "stray." The ex-Marine had no money and had been sleeping in a clothes bin in a shopping center where people left their old clothes to be distributed. He was dirty, hungry, and homeless. We had to outfit him and I brought out a favorite wool sweater of mine. The thought immediately came, *You have some old sweaters you can give, why this new one?* And my memory sped back to the linen sheets and mother's principle—"We give our best." It will be a continuing challenge to me the rest of my life.

A.THURBER

Sheep Amid Wolves

"Behold, I send you forth as sheep in the midst of wolves" (Matthew 10:16).

The sun had just dropped over the hills to the west. Soon it would be dark. The trucks were late. From the hill where I was watching I looked down to the corral, water tank, windmill, and pens below. There were horses tied to a fence. A great fire of live oak branches burned as the ranch hands prepared for the arrival of the new stock. The smell of the fire drifted toward me on the quiet evening air. Only an occasional neigh of a horse, or an order from the top hand could be heard. And then I saw a gleam of light in the distance. It would be the headlights of the lead cattle truck as it slowly navigated the rough, ungraded ranch road.

The year was 1941 and I had bought a ranch in Medina County, Texas. Now the first delivery of stock was arriving. My Grandmother Conant had died that spring and the proceeds from her bequest to me permitted me to buy the stock. I'd had to borrow to purchase the land. The previous week I had traveled to the county seat in Hondo and registered my brand, The Open A E ⌒E. The fee had been fifty cents. I had purchased branding irons and now the sheep were arriving. It was a terribly exciting moment for me.

Rocks rolled from the hill, my boots dislodging them, as I ran to be on hand when the first tailgate rattled to the ground. What a thrill it was to see the sheep with my brand upon them! From that day onward, whenever I saw a sheep, a steer or an angora goat I felt the satisfaction of seeing "my" brand. I guess it is a human weakness to want to see things labeled, catalogued, and branded for easy identification. Thomas stated, "Except I see in his hands the print of the nails, and put my finger into the print of the nails, and thrust my hand into his side, I will not believe" (John 20:25). Whether we like it or not, we are branded. Those about us are constantly evaluating us and, as Christians, we are being reviewed as to whether we reflect the love, the values, and the quality of life worthy of a disciple of Jesus Christ. We are on display. People want to see whose brand we wear.

As I bought wool, I learned more and more about sheep. I could see why the Old and New Testaments so often referred to us as sheep and the Lord as the Good Shepherd. Perhaps one of most difficult passages for me to understand was Matthew 10:16, "Behold, I send you forth as sheep in the midst of wolves: be ye therefore wise as serpents, and harmless as doves." Why would the Lord Jesus Christ, who personifies love to us and is indeed Love itself, make so heartless a statement as to send his sheep into a wolf pack? I saw the grisly remains of sheep and lambs attacked by coyotes. Could this statement have been made the way it sounds?

A sheep is nearly helpless to protect itself. It cannot climb trees, dig holes in the ground, run fast, fly, bite, kick effectively, camouflage itself, or claw. Its enemies are numerous and powerful. There are wolves, foxes, coyotes, eagles, mountain lions, and boars or javelinas. Matthew 10 prophesies all sorts of trials for the "sheep"—scourging, betrayal by family, persecution, and execution. It would be cruel—except for the promise to the sheep that he has a shepherd. Certainly domestic sheep would not exist except for their value to the shepherd. John 10 tells us that the Good Shepherd gives his life for the sheep, that he calls each sheep by name, that he is the door of the sheepfold through which the sheep is saved and goes in and out and finds pasture. Then there is the promise that they have eternal life and that no man can pluck them out of his hand. What would otherwise be callous abuse becomes a secure relationship because the sheep have the shepherd.

Texas is a fenced (closed) range. There are other areas of the West that have open range, and it is here that there are still shepherds. The shepherd has dogs to help control the movement of the sheep but he is often the only human being in a vast area. Many of these men have Basque origins. They know their charges well and are committed to their care.

One night in a rugged area where the snows were recently melted and the grass was just turning green, I spent an evening with a shepherd and his flock. There were two thousand sheep held on this lush mountainside for the night. The bonfire provided the means of preparing a good supper. Three dogs enjoyed bones near us. The sun had long since set and the vermillion sky had changed to burnt umber.

The sheep had quieted down, and then I heard it—the long wail of a coyote behind our camp. Across the arroyo was an answering call. The dogs looked pleadingly at the shepherd for his consent to find the coyotes. The shepherd knew this was what the coyotes would like as the sheep would then be deprived of their protection. The sheep were on their feet now, and there was some bleating as the ewes brought their lambs close. The shepherd tossed some large logs on the fire, and the flames rose. In this light I looked out and saw thousands of little lights. I realized that these were reflections of the fire in the eyes of the sheep. In the midst of danger the sheep were not looking out into the darkness but were keeping their eyes set in the direction of their safety, looking toward the shepherd. I couldn't help but think of Hebrews 12:1, 2,

> Wherefore seeing we also are compassed about with so great a cloud of witnesses, let us lay aside every weight, and the sin which doth so easily beset us, and let us run with patience the race that is set before us, looking unto Jesus the author

and finisher of our faith; who for the joy that was set before him endured the cross, despising the shame, and is set down at the right hand of the throne of God.

Looking unto Jesus! It was enough for the sheep, and I knew it would be enough for me.

Women Make Sacrifices, Too

Life contains many "small decisions" that, in retrospect, are the really great decisions of our lives. Each day is exciting, as it contains the time wherein these everyday decisions are made. At the end of each day we can have a sense of accomplishment, if we know that these decisions and the actions taken as a result of them are directed by the Holy Spirit. In counseling, Marian and I find that young people are looking for the great decision, often neglecting those smaller ones that develop discipline, performance, and values.

As an example of the importance of the "small" decision I often use the way in which most couples enter marriage. I know of one case where a sailor friend of mine came with me to the wool office on Summer Street in Boston. He made it as far as the receptionist. I wondered where he had gone, and I retraced my steps to find him talking with Leona Ott. He never did get to see the office. As we left and were walking over the Fort Point Channel Bridge, Bill said, "Allan, I'm going to marry that girl." Several months later they were married, and I was best man at their wedding. Generally, however, a man is introduced to a girl who may or may not immediately impress him. He makes the decision to ask her for a date. Other decisions follow, and often a couple is married without an official proposal. The "big" decision was the sum of many ordinary ones. This was the way it happened with Marian and me.

We met the first day of school at Wheaton College. The football field was limed out to be a giant map of the United States, and freshmen were asked to take their places in the approximate spot where they lived. Those from Texas had a hard time even talking together, but Marian Smith lived in Maine, and Massachusetts was really relatively close. I found out that this black-haired girl from Maine lived in a town called New Vineyard. Her town consisted predominantly of hardwood trees. I later learned that I failed to make much of an impression. Marian was in my Bible class and, while she was very quiet and retiring, she had all the answers. She never raised her hand when a question was asked by the professor, and only responded to direct questioning. When no one else had the answers the professor asked, "Miss Smith?" It was exasperating to have a classmate of this sort. With her long hair done up in a bun, she was very attractive. She dressed conservatively. But, she was friendly when addressed.

Upon the advice of the Assistant Dean of Women, who was a good friend of my sister Elsie, I invited Marian to a special function. She did not accept until she found that others with whom she would rather have gone failed to ask her. We had a good time. She says that her chief asset with me was that she was a good conversationalist—she listened. This probably was how it was. I was somewhat reluctant to date a girl who was obviously smarter than I. As I came to know her better, this disparity of mental ability vanished as we always talked about sailing, a sport not frequently followed in the deep woods of Maine. In later years, when our three children were in junior and senior high school, I made the statement that probably my greatest gift to the children was in marrying their mother so they could inherit her brains. Son Arthur immediately replied, "Yes, daddy, but think what brains we'd have had if you hadn't diluted the strain!" For the record—Arthur has not been disinherited.

I had left college to learn the wool business. My father was in his sixties and there was no one in the family to carry on. Edward, my brother, was a minister whose work was opening up closed churches in Vermont. Two of my three sisters were married to ministers. So, reluctantly, I left college to be an office boy in Emery and Conant Co., Inc., Wool Merchants. I loved the work, all sixty hours a week of it for $10 a week. It was fascinating. In two and a half years I had become a wool buyer in Texas and a salesman; I was making $35 a week, and I had purchased, by borrowing, some stock in the company.

Over the years Marian and I had written letters, she writing regularly every six months and I immediately replying. One day I received an invitation to visit her home in Maine. Thereafter, she would visit her sister Margaret, who lived in Boston, every month or two. She always let me know when she would be arriving.

Pearl Harbor came. I had my Sunday school boys out on a hike, and when we returned to the car we heard that Pearl Harbor had been bombed. Like others, I didn't even know where Pearl Harbor was. The next day I enlisted as an apprentice seaman in the regular U. S. Coast Guard. Our property was taken over by the Army for a searchlight antiaircraft site. Being on a high hill it commanded an excellent view of the harbor. Soldiers were billeted in the playhouse and sentries patrolled the drives. We were very conscious of war conditions. I expected to be called up immediately, so I sent a wire to Marian, "Have enlisted in the U. S. Coast Guard. Expect to be at sea shortly." The reply was, "Will be on afternoon train tomorrow."

At dinner that night mother expressed the belief that Marian was getting serious. She felt I should let Marian know that it would be a mistake to be married in wartime. I worked out the fine speech I would make during dinner the following night. It would keep my options open, not hurt her feelings, and make me appear rather noble. When you can do all these things in one paragraph you are doing well.

I picked Marian up at the train and we had dinner at the City Club. Our table looked out over the blacked-out port of Boston. We had a good dinner and then, after two deep breaths, I gave my speech. "Marian, you know that if a fellow were in love with a girl he wouldn't think of getting married in wartime as he has no way of knowing if he will come back whole, or at all. It just wouldn't be fair to the girl." I was quite proud of myself. Marian looked me straight in the eye and said, "If I were in love with a man, I'd rather be his wife and his widow than not his wife at all. Allan, in wartime women make sacrifices, too, and if a man had any regard, respect, and love for a girl, he would let her decide the sacrifices she was prepared to make." I could say nothing.

When I arrived at home, my mother and my youngest sister, Elsie, were at the door. Elsie was living at King Oak Hill as her husband, Newton Schoenly, was a chaplain in the Army. Elsie said, "How did it go?" I recited Marian's reply. Mother looked serious and said, "Allan, Marian is smarter than you. You are over your depth."

Six months later we were engaged. Two months after that we became man and wife. I have never ceased to be grateful to our great God who "doeth all things well" for giving me a life partner who was willing to accept responsibility, make sacrifices, and be an inspiration to her children and grandchildren, and, especially, to her husband.

North Atlantic, February 3, 1943

The day after Pearl Harbor found me at the Navy Recruiting Office in Boston. The line was interminably long, so Albert Baker, my fellow-worker at Emery & Conant Company, Inc., and I proceeded to the U. S. Coast Guard Recruiting Office, where we found an equally long queue but decided we might as well remain. Several hours later we had signed up as apprentice seamen, had our physical examinations, and were told we should soon receive reporting notice.

We did, and for me it was the cultural shock of my life. The first night in the barracks at Gallups Island was a nightmare. There was no discipline. Instead I heard profanity, obscenities, and loud tales of sex orgies. How long could I exist in this atmosphere? I read my Bible but didn't dare to kneel beside my cot, so I lay on my stomach and asked the Lord to take me Home soon and, if possible, gloriously. I had no faith that the God of miracles could touch lives such as those about me. Those were days of doing everything at once. We were given no "boot camp" training. One lad shot off his foot the first night he was issued a rifle for guard duty. We worked eight hours on—eight hours off. We were dirty, tired, and cold most of the time.

I had a bunk six tiers up, where a 300 watt light bulb hung two feet from my face and burned twenty-four hours a day. In spite of this, I would fall into the sack and "die" until the watch was called. One afternoon, shortly before I had to go on duty, a figure appeared climbing up the ladder by my bunk and a voice said, "Hey, whatcha readin'?" I replied, "My Bible." A laugh and then a shout, "Get a load of this, mates, Emery's readin' a Bible." Instantly a voice from one of the first level bunks replied, "It wouldn't do you any harm to read it yourself." I dropped down to see who had come to my defense and met a powerful lad who was at that moment reading from The Book of Common Prayer. His name was Richard Dane Phippen. We became friends at once, and today we serve together on the Board of Directors of three different organizations. He represented the very best example of patriotic commitment and Christian devotion. We went to church together whenever we had the opportunity, and we often indulged ourselves, after a patrol, in a marshmallow fudge sundae at Bailey's.

There was another sailor who stood out as particularly happy and enthusiastic. His name was Joseph Olzewski. Blond, slight but sturdy, he had a smile that revealed flashing white teeth. His home was in Baltimore, but other than this I knew little about him. By this time I had been assigned to the gate at Lewis Wharf, as one of four sailors acting as Quartermasters. This particular Friday night I was to be at my post from midnight till 0600. I hit the sack at seven in order to get some sleep before my watch. As I was undressing, Joe entered the watchkeepers' bunkroom. He was dressed in immaculate dress blues, his hat squared, the piping on his cuffs snow white, and his shoes spit-shined. He gave me his biggest smile and asked, "How do I look?" I replied, "You look beautiful, Joe. What's the big event?"

Joe excitedly explained that at the U.S.O. the previous night a society girl had invited him to spend the weekend with her at her apartment in Louisburg Square on Beacon Hill. She was taking him to the opera that night, and she had lots of records and liquor. He didn't have to report back to the base until 0700 Monday. "This is going to be the greatest time of my life." I told him I'd be praying for him. He walked out and immediately reentered the bunk-room. "What did you just say?" he demanded. "I said I'd be praying for you."

"Why will you be praying for me, when I'm going to have the first great weekend of my life?"

"Because, Joe, Monday morning you'll be back aboard and you will not be the same person you are tonight. Sin leaves its marks. The Bible says that there is pleasure in sin but it is only for a season and the results are spiritual death."

He swore at me and went out into the night. I prayed for Joe and the next thing I knew I was being called for the watch. I dressed, read the special night orders, and checked in the liberty party due at midnight and logged those overleave. Then I started walking my post in a "military manner" as the General Orders prescribed. The patrol craft tugged at their mooring lines in the basin. The flood-lights bathed the old warehouse area outside the heavy-duty fence, and all was quiet.

Some distance from the gate two boxcars stood awaiting the switch engine later in the day. As I walked back and forth in what I intended to be a "military manner" I caught a movement in my peripheral vision near one of the boxcars, just beyond the range of the flood lights. I continued to walk my post, keeping alert to the moving shadow. Then I saw the form of a man exposed in the lights. I gave the challenge, "Halt, who goes there?" No answer. "Advance and be recognized." And, to my amazement, I saw a sailor in dress blues walking toward me. It was Joe. He looked agitated, and he was not in a smiling mood. I asked, "Joe, what on earth are you doing here? I thought this was the big weekend when you were going to have a good time."

"How can you have a good time with someone praying for you?" he complained. "You've ruined my weekend. I stood up my date and I've been waiting until you came on duty and checked in the liberty party. Now, tell me how to find God."

We went into the sentry box, from where I could view

the gate, and I opened my New Testament and shared with Joe the great promises of the Lord Jesus Christ, including John 3:16. Joe had never heard the promises and scriptural assurance of forgiveness of sin and certain hope of eternal life. When he left to go to bed at 6 a.m., his smile was broader, his confidence greater, and his joy complete, for Joe had accepted Christ's salvation, freely offered, for himself for all eternity.

Everyone noticed the difference in Joe, and some felt it would pass away. Joe joined Park Street Church. Joe spent his free time on the Boston Common, inviting Service personnel to the services of the church, and he became himself a great recruiter for the Lord. When I came in from patrol, he would come to the house. He, and Dick Phippen, and I would go to St. Paul's Cathedral, which was always open for prayer. Joe had a fine voice and he loved to sing "You Are My Sunshine" in harmony. He learned hymns and sang them walking down the street. The base finally got the message that Joe had found something real.

Dick and I and others went to sea. Over the months Joe was promoted to Store Keeper Second Class and was stationed at headquarters at 40 Broad Street. It was great duty and allowed him to continue his missionary work on the Common, and to grow in his knowledge of Scripture by sitting under Dr. Harold John Ockenga. We corresponded. His last letter stated that he felt as if he were not doing his part, so he had applied for sea duty and would be leaving for his ship in a few days. The ship he sailed on was carrying mines for Reykjavik, Iceland, and three days out of New York a Nazi torpedo found her as a target and there were no survivors. I presume Joe died in one great explosion rather than in the icy waters of the North Atlantic.

Every Sunday as I leave the church sanctuary I pass a bronze plaque. The first name is that of "Joseph S. Olzewski S. K. 2/c U.S.C.G. Lost February 3, 1943 North Atlantic." I still see his happy smile, hear his clear voice singing the hymns of faith, and his excited recital of a lad who had just found Jesus Christ as his Savior. And I thank God for his memory and the reality of 2 Corinthians 5:17, "If any man be in Christ he is a new creature; old things are passed away. Behold all things are become new." I await that time when "the sea shall give up her dead and the corruptible bodies of them who sleep in Him shall be changed like unto His glorious body, according to the mighty working whereby He is able to subdue all things unto Himself" (Book of Common Prayer).

LOST AT SEA

U.S.C.G.

A. THURBER

You Have to Go Out. You Don't Have to Come Back

—Old Motto of the United States Lifesaving Service—

The winter of 1943 was an unusually bitter one on the New England Coast. I had been in the United States Coast Guard for over a year and had served in small craft in antisubmarine patrol and convoy activity most of that period. At the time of this experience I was a Boatswain's Mate First Class and "Officer-in-Charge" of an eighty-foot converted yacht. Much of our activity was routine, and my major concern was keeping my men from the dangers of liberty ashore rather than the perils of the deep.

We had been relieved on patrol off Block Island and had smashed our way through heavy northwesterly seas back to our mooring at the Newport Base. The wind continued to make up, and the seas roared against the shore even on the bay side of Aquidneck Point. All but one seaman and I left on liberty. I had gone without sleep the preceding night and was looking forward to an uninterrupted rest in my luxurious bed in what had been the owner's cabin.

Before hitting the sack, I made a final inspection of our mooring lines, decided to double them up, gave "night orders" to the "anchor watch" and dug into my wonderful bed. I'd had my devotions before retiring but even as I lay in my bunk I thanked the Lord that I was in harbor tonight and could sleep there. I enjoyed hearing the scream of the wind in the rigging while warm inside. The anemometer was indicating 40 knot winds with gusts to 55—gale velocity. The seas off the coast where the wind would have a fetch would be 20 feet.

I was about to drop off when I heard a footfall on the deck above me. A gust of wind invaded my cabin as the wheelhouse door was opened and quickly closed. A voice, still muffled, shouted, "Skipper aboard? Captain of the Port wants him on the sentry-box phone." I was on my feet and took time to put on a face mask before walking the length of the pier. The voice at the other end of the line said, "Emery, we have a Navy pilot who has gone down and you've got to go out." I reminded Captain Scott that I had just returned from a two-day patrol and that my men were on liberty. He replied that I could round them up in the taverns. I felt I should tell him that in 10° cold and gale winds no pilot could live but a few minutes. Through the roar of the wind outside the sentry-box I could clearly hear the officer shouting through the phone, "Emery, when the Coast Guard took over the U. S. Lifesaving Service they also accepted its motto, although only 'Semper Paratus' is used today. The motto is 'You have to go out, but you don't have to come back.'" All I could say is, "Aye, aye, sir." The crew was in one tavern, and all in the same state of almost total intoxication. The icy blast enroute to the ship seemed to steady them to the point they felt like going to bed.

We started up our engines, set a war cruising watch, and proceeded to the "gate" where a special signal answered the challenge. We had the wind and harbor chop on our starboard quarter, and we rode well. Ice was forming on our bow, and frozen spray and spindrift required keeping a port in the wheelhouse open. As soon as we were out of the lee of land we felt the full force of the gale. The sea seemed to have a personal vendetta against our vessel. Thus we proceeded to the latitude and longitude given as the spot where the plane ditched. There were no signs of wreckage. We patrolled slowly to save the ship from unnecessary battering. I had taken bearings to obtain a fix. Most navigation lights had been extinguished to enforce the blackout and to eliminate the "loom" against which coasting vessels could be sighted by enemy submarines. It was a clear night and bearings could be obtained against the still visible distant points of land.

Suddenly, a light shone bright and clear. It was a group flashing light. I checked my chart but saw no beacon, lighthouse, or flashing buoy in any location near this light. It was flashing three short, three long, and three short white flashes. All of us in the wheelhouse suddenly realized it was an S.O.S. We sent back the message on the blinker, "Stand by, we are coming." Increasing our speed, we changed course and headed straight for the light some four miles toward land. It appeared to be about the location of a reef, well out from the coast. Sure enough, we saw a small Navy craft, larger than we, its bow hard aground on the inshore side of the reef. The stern was almost awash and was taking a beating from the seas. We could not tow the vessel over the reef, so we would have to invade the dangerous waters ourselves to put a line aboard. The chart showed both rocks awash and rocks under the surface. We could well go aground ourselves. The grounded vessel could not last long, and no boat could take off the crew.

Several times we attempted to heave a "monkey's fist" aboard to carry a line, but the wind hurled it back aboard. I decided we had to get full to windward to pass a line. Since we drew only a fathom, we stood a chance of not going aground. The men got line, messenger, and towing hawser over and secured the hawser. I took a strain and then gave full power to haul the stranded vessel. Nothing happened. With my stern fixed, my bow was now acting as a sail and the seas and wind began to cause me to broach to. It was then I felt my keel aft hit. Now all that was left was for us, too, to break up. No help could come in time. We'd had to go out, but we did not have to come back. Others had done as we were doing. We had our orders, and had done our duty. In spite of the crashing of seas and roar of wind, the wheelhouse was still. I remember quietly telling the Lord that it was all right, but if he wanted anything more in the life of one Allan Emery and the men in these ships he'd have to move quickly. Our ship was helpless.

To the northwest the distant darkness that was land disappeared. I realized that a great sea was charging down upon us at express train speed. By reflex I gave the engines maximum power, and the sea lifted us like a cork. The hawser tightened, flinging water in all directions; our stern lifted, and we were free. Then, to our amazement, the same sea lifted the grounded vessel as in that moment the pull from our hawser hauled her loose. We towed her stern-to into deep water. She was leaking badly. We received word to secure our operation, and we returned to port with the battered ship in tow. Beaching her on a mud flat on the westerly side of Narragansett Bay so she wouldn't sink, we proceeded back to base.

As we were now able to think our own thoughts, I found myself asking the question, "The utter obedience required in the military is accepted as necessary, even when one's life may be the price of that obedience. Why does the Christian fail to practice the same obedience in spiritual matters?" I determined that with God's help I'd remember Captain Scott's words to me and apply them to my Christian duty. "You have to go out, but you don't have to come back."

As a note of interest, the Navy pilot had his position wrong. He ditched his plane just off Revere Beach, Massachusetts, and actually was able to walk ashore.

Log Them As Deserters!

"Very well, Mr. Craig*, log them as deserters," shouted the Captain. "Single up all lines."

"Engine Room, this is the Captain speaking. Stand by to answer all bells."

"Aye, aye, Captain. Standing by to answer all bells."

"Take in the after brow."

"Stand by to take in the gangway."

"But, Captain, you are not going to leave Mr. Emery and Mr. Gates, are you? We need these officers," protested Mr. Craig, the Executive Officer.

The bridge was strangely silent. Enlisted men and officers tensely awaited the response to the plea of Mr. Craig. With a roar the Captain bellowed, "I do not need the assistance of 'deserters.' Log them, sir! Take in lines 1, 3, 4, 5 and 6."

I had served under Commander Cranmer* (the title of Captain is given to any commanding officer of lower rank) for nearly a year as one of 15 officers and 230 men who comprised the complement of the *U.S.S. Faulkner**in World War II. The present cruise had begun several days earlier, when we had received orders to lead our squadron to a

---

* Names of personnel and ships have been changed.

rendezvous, 10 miles east of the sea buoy off Cape Henry, with a Task Group of Attack Transports (AKA's) we were to escort to the invasion of what were then to us unknown islands of the Southwest Pacific. We had arrived at the rendezvous well before the AKA's were picked up on radar. The C.I.C. (Combat Information Center) reported the bearing of the ships, and lookouts competed to be the first with the cry, "Sail ho." There was much excitement as the blinkers sent messages between the Task Group Commander in *U.S.S. General John Stark** and the Escort Commander, Captain Riles,* in our own vessel. Captain Riles was given the complimentary term of "The Commodore" by our Captain Cranmer.

Shortly we took station ahead of the transports and headed south toward Cape Hatteras. We found the seas making up as we proceeded. Some new hands taken aboard at Norfolk were seasick, and one yeoman who was always seasick in heavy weather sat faithfully at his desk in the ship's office with his pail beside him. In the radio shack the watch was manning the many frequencies required and maintaining radio silence. I was on the bridge when the Communication Officer handed the Captain a message, "Hurricane approaching Florida Straits. Stand by for possible orders to proceed to Charleston." As we looked astern to the great transports laden with Marines, supplies, and equipment, we could see the landing craft rigged all along the sides of these ships. We knew that a hurricane could make kindling out of these exposed and vital boats. On the other hand, there was also a risk of security if our Task Group was directed into port. Two hours later we received word to proceed into Charleston, South Carolina.

The transports "dropped the hook" in the roadstead and the escorts proceeded to the Naval Operating Base where we berthed, nested with *U.S.S. Faulkner* inboard next to the long pier. A giant crane placed a gangway to our side as soon as we were secured, and our squadron was placed on a one-hour standby. We were to be prepared to sail within one hour of receiving orders.

Captain Thomas Cranmer had been in the service for fifteen years. Since his graduation from the Academy he had served both ashore and at sea, and had found promotion slow until war was declared. He had commanded a tug, a minesweeper, and now had the honor of a destroyer class vessel. Whether it was fear or the responsibility of command that effected the change we all saw developing in the Captain, we did not know. We did find him to be more and more petulant, demanding, accusing, self-pitying, and suspicious.

Sometimes he would awaken the officers at night to meet with him in the wardroom. Once he told us we slept too much, that four hours sleep was enough for Eleanor Roosevelt and it would be enough for us. He would have his steward check on each one of us and awaken us when we had had our maximum four hours. He told us not to apply for transfer as we could only get off the *Faulkner* by being sent to Portsmouth Penitentiary or by "the deep six" (over the side). He cut off officers' showers and had us notified when a rain squall was approaching so we could gather on the forecastle deck, naked with soap and washcloth. We could wet down, but there was never enough rain to rinse us off. The crew were amused as they watched their officers being disciplined by the Captain. The threats and deprivations merely brought officers and men closer. One lunchtime the Captain glowered at his officers and softly purred, "I hear that some of my officers are referring to my ship as 'a hell ship.' If that is what you say, by _____ I'll make it a 'hell ship'!" The last words were screamed. The stewards serving us were as shocked as we.

The summer countryside beyond the huge naval base at Charleston was inviting. Oh, to lie on the grass and watch the clouds sail past and sleep! As I walked forward I found my friend, Lieutenant Gates, sitting atop a bitt. We referred to him affectionately as "Pearly" and I knew how he must be longing to call his wife as she, like my wife Marian, was about to have a baby. Even if we were to be granted special permission to go ashore, we could not break security with a phone call. " 'Pearly,' do you suppose Mr. Craig would give us liberty to go to the Ship's Service Store at the base? We'll be at sea for so long. This could be our last chance to shop." He leaped up and we ran to the Exec's quarters. Mr. Craig smiled and said, "We are on one hour standby, but I'd be glad to give you a half-hour when the three officers I have let ashore return—provided, of course, we have not received orders to sail at that time." It was 1010 and the three officers were due back at 1020. We returned to the forecastle to watch for them. As soon as they appeared we presented ourselves to the Executive Officer once more and asked for the promised half-hour leave. He asked if the other officers had returned. We replied they had. "Very well, gentlemen, be aboard by 1050." "Aye, aye, sir. Thanks."

If we had not been limited by time and money we could have returned with all kinds of booty, for we found a world of scarce articles at the Ship's Service Store. We were watching the time carefully. At 1035 we both decided we should head back. The pier was long and we had spent one-half of our time. As we rounded a warehouse we could see the masts of our ship but, to our horror, we realized that the masts of those other ships moored outboard of us were not there. "Let's go, 'Pearly,' " I shouted, and we raced down the long pier.

It was 1031 when orders were received for the squadron to sail. Quarters for Muster was called; the Special Sea Detail set; the Executive Officer reported to the bridge, where the Captain sat in his elevated chair, "All ship's company present and accounted for. Mr. Emery and Mr. Gates are ashore and will be aboard by 1050." It was now 1040.

The Commodore was a quiet, taciturn man, businesslike, professional, and the kind of officer who inspires confidence. One word of praise from him was an event not to be forgotten. You knew you had earned it. His responsibility was the tactical command of the squadron, and often that of Convoy Commander and Task Group Commander. He had, however, no authority over the internal operation of the ship. This was the Captain's domain, and prerogatives were carefully observed.

While the ship was preparing to get under way, the Commodore had quietly taken his chair, located above and abaft the Con atop the sonar hut. He seldom came topside, and if he did, he sat in the Captain's chair, a cause of much frustration to the Captain. Since the Captain was in his chair the Commodore, unobserved by the Captain, was seated where he could see and hear all that was being done.

"What do you mean, two of my officers ashore when we are on immediate standby? They have jumped ship."

"No, Captain," Mr. Craig answered, "I gave them my permission to go to the Ship's Service Store for a half-hour. They are due back in nine minutes. They will be back."

"No Executive Officer of mine would give permission to any officer to go ashore when we are on immediate standby. You are trying to protect these men, sir. I will not have it. Log them as deserters!"

"Mr. Craig, order the gangway up." The giant crane dwarfed the operator high above our bridge, his head out of his cab window awaiting the signal to take up the heavy gangway. Mr. Craig looked pleadingly at the Captain. The Captain shouted, "Mr. Craig, I have given you a simple order to raise the gangway. Will you give this command, or will you force me to do it myself?"

Mr. Craig walked slowly to the port bridge wing, his hand half raised to signal the crane operator. He turned, a smile on his face. The Captain saw the smile and was enraged. "Mr. Craig, give the order, sir!"

"But, Captain, you don't want to leave the Commodore, do you?"

The Captain went to the rail, and there at the pier end of the gangway stood the Commodore. "Pearly" and I were running up the pier, and there at the gangway was the Commodore. The gold braid on his hat and the insignia on his collar flashed in the sun. We saluted. He returned the salute, and briskly followed us aboard. The gangway was lifted. It was 1047.

The Commodore had done the one thing he could do for us and for the ship. He did not interfere with tradition, but he simply left his chair, came down the ladders to the main deck, and walked off the ship to hold it for us. Thus he did for us what we could not do for ourselves, saving our reputations. He kept us from dishonor.

As I went to my stateroom I suddenly saw the principle of redemption in a new way. I saw the Lord Jesus Christ "being made sin for us who knew no sin; that we might be made the righteousness of God in him" (2 Cor. 5:21). I remembered 2 Corinthians 8:9, "For ye know the grace of our Lord Jesus Christ, that though he was rich, yet for your sakes he became poor, that ye through his poverty might be rich."

Last summer I traveled a long way to see the Commodore. Before his retirement, he had become a Rear Admiral. I thanked him for what he had done for me over thirty years before. He had actually forgotten the incident until I reminded him of it. As long as I live I shall remember his standing at the gangway to save us from disgrace, and with this memory be reminded of the Lord of Glory coming down to this world to die on a cross to save sinners like me from death and hell—and to provide us with eternal fellowship with himself.

Membership

"There is neither Jew nor Greek, there is neither bond nor free, there is neither male nor female; for ye are all one in Christ Jesus" (Galatians 3:28).

Thirtieth Street Station Philadelphia was as usual a scene of movement and activity. As I stood on the designated platform for "The Washington Express" I had time to notice those about me. A mother held a baby in her arms. An active three-year-old was being restrained from falling over the edge of the platform. All about this woman were suitcases and boxes. I knew she'd need help in boarding. A husband and wife had not spoken a word to each other for the ten minutes I had been waiting. How could people with years of common experience fail to share feelings and hopes and ideas? I watched the soldiers and sailors and believed I could tell which ones were headed home on leave and those who were enroute to their posts or ships.

Behind my conscious thoughts was the heaviness of heading off on a two-week selling trip. I liked selling, but today my two calls had been fruitless. New York was not buying cloth. I thought of Marian and her having to handle the affairs at home as well as our three children. There would be snowstorms, perhaps a power failure, and certainly inter-sibling disputes to arbitrate. How much happier it would be to be heading home, but the trip was just beginning and my responsibility now was to sell and service my customers who were also my friends.

Through all these thoughts I was conscious of something lifting my sagging spirits. It was not the raw wind blowing through the vaultlike caverns of the train platforms. There was no cheerful smile to brighten the gray, darkening day.

Suddenly I realized that there was a beautiful whistling over the public address system. I knew the song. It was "How Great Thou Art." The words formed in my mind as the whistling continued. Where was the whistler? I looked about. Three minutes more before my train would be rushing into the station. Leaving my sample cases and bag, I raced up the stairs. I asked the station master's assistant where the train announcer was. Then I ran down the stairs to the platform indicated, and there in a small glass cubicle was the whistler, a black man, perhaps thirty years old. I smiled, and he nodded his head. The whistling ended abruptly. He announced: "The Washington Express," and its platform and the position of Pullman cars and coaches distinctly and authoritatively backed up his claim. The rush and roar of the train, the scream of brakes confirmed the announcement. Then I had to run back up to the concourse and down to the platform for my train. I waved, and the whistler waved while he was still announcing—but in that brief interchange there was membership. I had shared my appreciation, and he knew he had been a blessing to a fellow-believer and member of the family of God.

My bags were taken in quickly by the porter. The woman with the baby and little boy were aboard, and the small lad already had his nose pressed flat against the window. I relaxed in the warmth of the Pullman. The train picked up speed as it rattled over switches, but now I was at peace. The Lord had used the witness of the Christian train announcer to bless me and to remind me that we are never alone. God has his people and there is that bond between them that revives the sagging spirit and confirms the love of God.

Membership is mentioned as the third level by Maslow in his hierarchy of human needs. The world attempts through secret societies, exclusive clubs, social groups and organizations to promise a sense of membership. There certainly are needs provided in these groups, but nothing compared to the membership of Believers. Believers know they are children of the King, that they have a common cause, a unique relationship to God and to one another, and a future in the presence of God. That announcer knew that somehow we "belonged." And now I could see this trip, not as an interruption in my family life but a part of his purpose in training me and using me in his service. I just asked the Lord to let me be like my brother the announcer and be a blessing.

Some years later I was on a round-the-world wool buying trip with one of my customers. The trip took three months. We were in Christchurch, New Zealand, at the United Service Hotel in Cathedral Square. I had been valuing wool in the wool warehouses since daybreak and now I returned to my room to code a cable to send to the Boston office. The door of my room was ajar, and a small white sign was on the floor outside that had the word "Electrician" stenciled on it. I went to my desk and started to work. The electrician was evidently working in the bathroom. I was deeply concentrating on my coding when I found myself following the tune being whistled by the man in the bathroom. I stopped. I knew the song well but I couldn't put a handle on it. I walked into the bathroom and there, flat on his back, was the electrician. I introduced myself and asked the name of the song he was whistling. He smiled and replied, "I Will Sing of My Redeemer." Of course, that was it. I stated, "You must be a Christian." He replied, "I am. I saw your Bible on the table by your bed and thought you might like to come to our home tonight where we have a prayer meeting. I didn't know how else to approach you as a guest except by whistling a hymn." Membership! Instant membership! God always has his way of building the body of Christ. This is the church.

Some years later I was staying at the Menzies Hotel in Melbourne. John Glenn would be orbiting the earth that night. The city of Perth was leaving its lights on and all

Australia was at high pitch for the event. I left a call for 7 a.m. and, as is the custom there, tea, toast, rolls, and butter are delivered to one's bedside at the time of call. I was awakened by a knock on the door and the turn of a key. An elderly chambermaid walked briskly toward my bedside table to place the tea tray. My Bible was there and as I removed the Bible she said, " 'Tis a precious Book and it speaks of a precious Man." Her thick Scottish accent was evident and her Christian faith confirmed. She told me of John Glenn's passing over and of her prayers for him. Every time we passed in the corridors of the hotel thereafter we exchanged greetings and shared briefly of what God was doing in our lives. Here again was instant "membership"! We were pilgrims enroute to the Celestial City. We were members of the body of Christ and we knew it.

More recently I was in Paris on business. The hotel was not deluxe but my room was adequate for the two nights I had to spend there. The "jet lag" reduced my sleep to four hours, and by the time I returned to my small quarters I was feeling sorry for myself. The room was neat and tidy and my bed turned back. Upon my Bible, which I had apparently left open, was a note. It said, "It is very nice. I'm a child of God as you." There was sketched a picture of a chambermaid complete with a feather duster. This woman was off duty the next day when I left and I shall not see her this side of heaven, but I rejoiced in God's encouragement to me through her.

On planes, ships, at filling stations, restaurants, and in business conferences, I have met those whom I knew to be brothers and sisters in Christ. There was that same immediate sense of unity, the ability to communicate on the deepest levels and the comfort of belonging. Jesus said (John 15:15), "Henceforth I call you not servants; for the servant knoweth not what his lord doeth: but I have called you friends." The intimacy which we have as friends of Jesus is available to help us be friends with each other.

It's very nice!
I'm a child of
God as you.

Abandon Ship, All Hands!

"For whosoever will save his life shall lose it; and whosoever will lose his life for my sake shall find it" (Matthew 16:25).

Hurricanes and whole gales are a part of sailing the North Atlantic in winter. My memory majors on the bone-chilling cold of long watches, the gnawing fears of whether the ship could further sustain the battering of the seas, of collision, of fire, and, of course, enemy action. The most wearying of all was fighting the violent motion of the ship itself. There was never a moment of rest. At meals we tied the arms of our chairs to the table. At night we often tied ourselves under the covers to keep from being hurled out of our bunks.

Many has been the night I have lain in my quarters listening to the war of the seas—separated from it by only 9/16ths of an inch of steel. The creaks and groans of the vessel as she worked through mountainous waves have assailed my ears. I have heard the scream of the gale in the rigging, the hurried dogging of hatches, the muffled movement of men as the watch changed, but ever the war of the seas goes on against the ship. There can be peace in such experience. You develop a trust and a confidence in your ship and its ability and strength to survive the tempest and the fury of the storm. Inherent to every ship is the possibility of its sinking.

I enjoy reading the advertising of cruises. The layout

speaks of the comfort of the staterooms, the superb cuisine, the ship's recreational opportunities, the splendor of the public rooms, the entertainment, the social opportunities, the glamor, and exotic ports-of-call. Even the number of bars and swimming pools is listed. I have yet to see any mention of the number of lifeboats the ship carries, their comfort, ease of loading, their food and water supplies, or their chance of being lowered away in heavy weather or if the ship is listing badly.

Lifeboats are not advertised because they admit the possibility of the ship having to be abandoned. Is it possible to imagine greater safety in a little boat than in the luxury of a great liner? If there were a way of hiding lifeboats this might help sustain the false assumption that the ship is indeed a "floating hotel." Lifeboats are tested, men trained in their use, and passengers looking very undignified in their lifejackets have to take part in lifeboat drills.

The *Titanic,* the "unsinkable" White Star Liner, struck an iceberg on 15 April, 1912 and began to sink immediately. The alarm was given. Passengers continued to dance. The orchestra played. The order was given to "Abandon ship," but the first boats went away empty. People dressed in evening clothes couldn't believe they should leave the warmth, luxury, and comfort of the beautiful ship for the discomfort and cold wetness of a little boat. More than 1500 passengers lost their lives—some because there were not enough boats, some because they wouldn't leave soon enough.

The Lord Jesus Christ tells us if we close our hot little fists over anything we are going to lose it. Our Lord teaches that we are simply stewards of what he gives—health, intellect, family, friends, material possessions and the time allotted to us in this life. We save and lose; we lose and save.

One of our young people made a trip to a missionary station where he met a fine young girl for whom he felt a strong attachment. When he left, the girl gave him a rose as a reminder of their friendship. He was in love, and he carried this beautiful flower in his left fist for the whole thirty-six-hour return trip to Boston. Upon his arrival he told Marian and me of all that had happened and of the beautiful flower he had been given. He then opened his hand and to his horror the flower was now something to be disposed of quickly. We see children held too tightly by parents. We see possessions strangling the possessors.

Son Allan explained to us, as he viewed his own life in the light of Galatians 2:20, "For one who is crucified with Christ, hanging on a cross there is no comfortable future; no career plan. There is the freedom of being with Christ, sharing his cross, and the joy of facing an eternity with him."

We each have our own ways to abandon ship. God speaks to us in different ways to surrender different things to make us free. To a seaman the text is simple enough. It is the solemn, urgent command—"Now hear this: Abandon Ship, All Hands!"

Final Witness

To us five children, daddy represented strength, security, wisdom, loving concern, responsibility, authority, justice, and a living example of Christian life and witness. As I have stated earlier, we knew him to be fallible. He sometimes became ill; he lost his cool at times when driving; he raised his voice when a clerk, taxi driver or hotel cashier in a foreign country did not understand his English. I remember a waiter in Berlin who brought him hot tea when he had clearly asked for "iced tea." Daddy tried to be patient but asked again for "iced tea" and the waiter brought him tea even hotter. The problem was solved when the head waiter, who understood English, explained that the waiter thought "iced" meant "heiss" (hot).

These occasional glimpses of daddy's failings somehow made his qualities of character stand out more clearly. We knew he was human and as subject to all the temptations of flesh and spirit as we. This gave us hope that the same God whom he served could work in our lives the miracles of grace necessary to bring us victory.

It was just before Elsie and Newt were married when Hitler and Stalin invaded Poland. For years the media had kept us aware of the ambition of Hitler. Mother, dad, Elsie, and I had been in Great Britain in 1938 during the "Munich Crisis" and had been issued gas masks. We had seen the air raid shelters being constructed in parks, under hotels, and along highways. In spite of Chamberlain's famous "Peace in our time" quote, we knew war was inexorably approaching. My draft number was low, but I knew eventually I'd become involved.

Edward and Mel Rowbotham were too old to go. David Fuller also was out of the age category, but he went in as a Navy Chaplain. Newt Schoenly and I were the ones involved, and daddy and mother read every news headline with us in mind. The day of reporting for duty arrived.

Daddy got up early and drove me to the Water Street Recruiting Office of the U. S. Coast Guard. As we approached he said, "Allan, I have been deeply involved in all you have done. I remember the first day you went to school, the day when you shipped on the *Swordfisherman Monhegan* for the summer, the day you and Bobby Bunce left for the summer in Canada and, of course, I followed your going to West Texas as a young wool buyer, and, later, your experiences as you traveled the South as a salesman. You are now going into a situation where I have had no experience myself, and I can't follow you in the same way. I can't call you on the phone. You will face new problems and dangers. But, what I can assure you is that the Lord Jesus will never leave you and that my prayers will be constantly with you." We rode the next few minutes in silence, as we neither dared to risk the tears further conversation would have caused.

I had only seen daddy cry once before, and that was when my sled dog Bruno had crawled home, having been hit by a neighbor who didn't even stop. That night Bruno was in great pain. All he could move was his tail, and when I came into mother's room where we had him on blankets, he would thump his tail. I held his head in my arms. When daddy came to call me for dinner and saw us there together on the floor, he just said, "Allie Boy, I guess you'd rather be here." And then his eyes filled, and for the first time, I saw him break into tears.

Years later I asked him why he never cried. He said that when his father died (he was just sixteen), he cried so much he decided that he could not let himself give in to tears.

This early morning, in the quiet darkness of the wartime streets of Boston, daddy nearly cried, and I felt as if he probably did cry after I left the car. We shook hands and I didn't look back. There was never a doubt that hour by hour through those long war years my parents prayed for Newt and me. When the sailors on the Boston docks and bases did not have winter underwear, daddy bought enough for us all and had the garments distributed through the Red Cross.

Daddy later developed rheumatoid arthritis. It was in his feet, knees, hips, arms, hands, shoulders, and he had to carry a rubber doughnut to sit upon. He was never without pain, except when asleep, for the last ten years of his life. I believe his attitude through all the suffering gave credibility to his Christian witness.

The Lord gave our parents a wonderful fiftieth wedding anniversary. The ninth of October, 1952, was a beautiful day, and friends were invited to a reception at King Oak Hill. There was even a hurdy-gurdy for atmosphere. The air was clear and fine from the northwest and we could see across the bay to Cape Ann. All the children were home for the occasion, and grandchildren ran about enjoying the food and each other.

Six weeks later I had just had a long telephone conversation with daddy when the phone rang. It was mother and she said, "Something has happened to daddy. Will you come over?" I raced the four miles to the house and saw at once that daddy had suffered a stroke. He was slumped in his wing chair, his face distorted, his eyes questioning, and his spirit even then triumphant. I carried him to the big sofa before the fire and finally located a doctor who would come. Daddy never left that room. We had a hospital bed, nurses around the clock, and let all who wanted to see him spend time with him. Daddy did not recover his speech nor movement in his hands. He could move his head and his eyes and the fingers of one hand. In this way he let me know of his commitments in his real estate interests. He also found ways to have us pray for those for whom he had special concerns. Two weeks later he had another stroke and remained in a semi-comatose state until he died on December 18th.

The night of his death I stayed at King Oak Hill, as we knew his time was short. I was still awake in bed when the nurse called and we went down to be with him. I stood by his bed as his breathing became shallower, and then he breathed his last. I turned to mother and said, "He's gone." Mother smiled and said, "What excitement at the 'Eastern Gate' there must be. Now, if you children will let me go upstairs alone for ten minutes, I'll come down and plan the funeral arrangments." I called the undertaker.

That night the family doctor, who was raised as an Orthodox Jew, said to me before leaving, "To me the final test of a man's theology is how it measures up to death. If you'll give me a New Testament, I'll read it carefully."

Daddy had wanted his will to have a witness, so he had copied into its preamble a statement he had read. It went like this:

> I commit my Soul into the Hands of my Savior in full confidence that, having redeemed it and washed it in his Most Precious Blood, He will present it faultless before the Presence of my Heavenly Father; and I entreat my children to maintain and defend at all hazards and at any cost of personal sacrifice the blessed doctrine of complete atonement for sin through the Blood of Jesus Christ once offered and through that alone.

As an executor of his estate, I thought of the lawyers, court clerks, and the judge who had to read this statement, and I realized this was a final witness. And now, as I write, I see that his final witness is written in the hearts and lives of children, grandchildren, and the host of those whom his life touched directly and indirectly, and will influence until our Lord returns.

When You Sell Out, You Always Sell Out Cheap!

I suppose that if there were a truism remembered by Bible clubbers more than any other, it would be this. I don't remember if this, too, was an expression used by my father, but I do know from life experience it is invariably true. It is so apparent to Marian and me when one of our clubbers "sells out." Often it is a small compromise—an association, a laugh at a comment made about another clubber, a matter of dress or conformity, the giving up of personal devotions, or an attitude toward parents and authority. I have never known of a person who suddenly determines to sell out his ethics or moral convictions, and sees the disastrous consequences of this decision.

Today's newspaper headlined the liquidation of one of the oldest and most prestigious of Boston businesses. My father and the father of the present principal of the business were close friends. It is difficult to imagine the suffering involved in this deliberate business decision. I am sure it will prove to be a wise one. Market changes necessitated making this judgment just as we had decided to liquidate our wool business. The personal sell-out of which I am speaking is seldom, if ever, viewed in sober analysis of alternatives as the kind of selling out denoted in today's newspaper. When a person sells his honor, virtue, integrity or faith, he has persuaded himself that the gain is all his. The enemy of his soul has helped him prepare his rationalization.

Adam and Eve expected to gain wisdom and pleasure and knowledge and experience from eating the forbidden fruit, but they immediately hid from God and viewed their own nakedness. At the time Jacob's tempting pottage seemed a good trade for Esau's birthright. Samson's revelation of his source of strength appeared justified to arrest the nagging of Delilah. He never saw that the end meant blinded eyes and becoming a beast of burden in the grist mill of a prison.

The Prodigal Son saw the adventures and the pleasures in a far-off country, but not the hunger and rejection that finally drove him to come home. Herod Antipas viewed the loss of face in failing to keep his promise to Salome. He never saw this as the final dissolution of character that would face him with the head of John the Baptist on a platter and win for himself an interview with the Lord Jesus, at which Jesus refused to speak to him. Pilate decided against the possible displeasure of Emperor Tiberius and ordered the crucifixion of the Lord of Glory. Judas wanted the security thirty pieces of silver could bring, and within a few hours he threw them away and hanged himself.

The Scriptures are replete with such illustrations, and so is life. Think of one person who made a good deal with the devil. If you come up with one, you either do not know the whole story or you haven't waited for the last chapter.

I think of real life "sell-outs"—ones ending in a car chase and the blast of troopers' bullets, of the long, sad marriage, the loss of profession in exchange for a moment of pleasure, and a cell in exchange for integrity.

Benedict Arnold has always fascinated me. He was a man of enormous ability, courage, and ambition. His expedition to Quebec in 1775 is an epic of leadership. His naval battle on Lake Champlain gained needed time for the American cause. He is seldom viewed as the real victor in the Battle of Saratoga. There is a monument to him on the battlefield that records no name and only his wounded bootleg is chiseled in stone. His name is synonymous with treachery and treason because he sold the fortification plans of West Point to the British for gold and rank. His last years were tragic ones, lived out in London in financial distress and mental anguish. From his diary I'd like to quote the last entries:

> April 19th. I have been very ill again—at death's door, they tell me, and out of my mind . . . . I have called for these memoirs again, to dedicate them to the American people . . . . But I cannot change them much . . . .
>
> June 12th. I have made a private memorandum for my personal belongings—the sword-knots, etc.,—and I have called Sage to get them with the Continental uniform . . . .
> "The old blue and buff one?" said the stupid English fool . . . . I said, Yes, and I looked at it a long time; it had one rip in the skirt I got at Ridgefield . . . . James, thinking it too shabby, was for getting a smart scarlet one. I told him No. I fell asleep, and he must have put it away . . . .
>
> June 13th. It is the only uniform I have ever worn with honor, and I would be buried in it . . . . Sage has left me . . . .
>
> June 14th, 1801. (Note by an unknown hand, probably Miss Fitch): —General Arnold expired at half past six this morning. His last moments were unconscious, but at dawn he was heard calling to his body-servant, Sage. He lay across the bed, half dressed, his lame leg in the buff breeches, the other still unclothed, as if he had fainted while drawing it on; on his body an old blue coat they told me had been his American uniform.

Here we see remorse, if not repentance. We see the final chapter never contemplated by the author when he sold out.

In spite of disappointments in the lives of some of those young people with whom Marian and I have spent much time, we have seen what true repentance can do to restore a relationship with God and to renew an effective witness. God is always available, always waiting, ever lovingly wooing the lost one back. What a reunion it is when the one who was lost is found!

Luke 15:24, "For this my son was dead, and is alive again; he was lost, and is found."

Dried Up Brooks

"And it came to pass after a while, that the brook dried up . . ." (1 Kings 17:7).

The flight had arrived late and it was midnight before I checked into the hotel of a southern city. It had been an eighteen-hour day, and as I prepared for bed I was tired and discouraged. I doubt if I have ever felt depressed, but I have often been deeply discouraged and never more so than this night. Tomorrow I should be calling upon my best customer, but he had retired as the chief executive officer of the mill and I had every reason to believe I would be displaced as a major supplier. As I unpacked, I laid my Bible on the night stand and decided that for once I'd go to bed without reading it. I was saying my prayers when, in frustration, I pled, "Lord, if You have something to say to me, some encouragement, let me have it now." I then opened my Bible and read a passage I had read many times before, but a new truth was presented to me. I went to sleep knowing that God had given me a promise and that tomorrow would be in his hands.

Elijah has always been my favorite Old Testament personality. His qualities of strength, fearlessness, faithfulness, and uncompromising obedience to God in the midst of enemy country are so vividly and dramatically displayed upon the pages of Scripture that I can see him as a real-life character.

Ahab, the king of Israel, was following in the idolatry and wickedness of his father Omri. Encouraging him in his sin was his wife Jezebel, the daughter of the regicide Ethbaal, king of the Zidonians. We first glimpse Elijah striding into the palace of Ahab and unceremoniously pronouncing the judgment of drought upon the land and abruptly turning on his heel. God spoke to Elijah and told him to head east, to hide by the brook Cherith, and that there ravens would feed him. He obeyed, and he was safe from the fierce anger of the king. But then one morning Elijah found the brook dried up. Some day I'll ask him what his thoughts were. Scripture does not tell us. There are several human reactions: (1) to view this as God's loss of interest in you, (2) to question the leading of the Lord to the brook, (3) to question God's power, and (4) to question his reality.

There are also several options we have relating to subsequent action. We can (1) go to the nearest tavern and get drunk; (2) go back to Ahab and give ourselves up—we can sell out to the enemy; (3) take Job's wife's advice and "curse God and die"; or (4) wait for the next command of God, knowing that by his character and by our life experience with him, we can trust him. He does not lead us into box canyons. As Marion Wade used to say, "God does not mock us."

We all have had "Dried Up Brooks." It may have been financial reverses, loss of friends and family, or health problems. We ask, "Why, Lord?" We see in our story one who submitted and was rewarded with a new and greater assignment, a future of being the Prophet of God and the means of keeping before a godless king and society the standards of the Lord.

In the twenty years since that night I have had numerous "Dried Up Brooks," but my attitude toward them has been one of expectancy, for I know God is faithful to me just as he was to Elijah. One experience was the long, drawn-out period of seeing the wool business dry up. My father had entered the wool business as a clerk-janitor in 1892. His father had died at the age of 57 and left nothing but debts and a little life insurance. The family lived in a large home and were used to a high standard of living. They were forced to take in boarders. My father moved to the attic to make room, and contributed by raising chickens and going to work in the leather business at $4.00 a week. A short time later he transferred to wool at the same salary. He was ambitious, hard-working, and a natural salesman. But he resented having to leave school and his lack of formal education made him an avid reader and gave him a continuing thirst for knowledge. His rise in the wool business was swift. He became a partner in Goodhue, Studley & Emery. A. D. Ellis and Cyril Johnson, two of his customers, each loaned him $25,000 at 4 percent interest to let him buy into the firm. The notes were repaid in two years. He built a business that specialized in fine quality wools, especially from Texas. The firm changed its name to Studley & Emery, Emery and Conant, and then to Emery, Russell & Goodrich, Inc. I entered the business in May of 1938 as an office boy at $10 a week for a 60-hour week. The law soon changed the standard work week to 48 hours and the minimum wage brought my salary to $11 a week. I was grateful even though the raise was not a "merit increase."

It was a good business; the ethical standards of the industry were extremely high. Contract was by word. Men kept their promises. There were elements of risk involved in every decision. The war years brought scarcity of fibre, manpower, and enormous taxes. I was away in the Service, but upon the cessation of hostility, the destitute world looked to this country for cloth. Ex-servicemen were buying civilian clothes. The mills were busy. After the post-war needs were met the Korean crisis brought government contracts for uniform cloth and blankets. Simultaneously the Congress decided to stockpile wool. This skyrocketed the price of wool.

My father did not follow the market. He felt that wool was artificially high and as a matter of principle, he told us, "We will never be in an inventory situation where we will want a war to continue to bail us out of our holdings."

This policy saved us. When the bubble burst, many wool merchants and mills closed their doors. Synthetics were now price-competitive with wool. Small mills were taken over by combines. Foreign competition, particularly from Japan, made many domestic manufacturers give up. We were faced with rising costs, a shrinking market, reduced margins of profit, and smaller commissions.

My father died in 1952, but we carried on profitably. Each year required doing more business with fewer customers. We had a great team, loyal buyers, and excellent credit, but the future looked grave. To liquidate a company while still profitable is a difficult decision to make. During those years I asked the Lord for wisdom, a vision, an angel, a Bible verse, anything to give me direction. I have always felt that finding the will of God in decision-making is the most difficult part of the Christian life.

One May noon I was in the dining car on the Pennsylvania Railroad, enroute from Baltimore to Philadelphia, and the Lord put this question to me: "If you were in the position of the minority stockholders of the company, knowing what you know about the future prospects of the wool business, would you want your assets in money instead of stock?" This involved the Golden Rule, and I decided to liquidate. I called a meeting of the Directors for the next morning to schedule a special meeting of the stockholders and to recommend liquidation. There was real consensus. Since daddy had set up a profit-sharing plan, employees would have funds with which to either retire or to live until they could find other employment. We liquidated at a good time for the stockholders and all our people found good employment, except one who retired.

There was never a question about this decision. I bought out a subsidiary, Emery Wool Company, and for five years continued in wool in a much smaller operation and with reduced expenses. But then I could see further withering of the industry and decided to leave the field completely. Then the question I raised was, "Why, God, did You lead me into a business with no future? Why all the waste of technical knowledge I have painfully acquired?" And the assurance came that "Dried Up Brooks" are a period in a sentence. The next sentence begins with a capital letter.

Decisions should be made in principle. Details can follow. There was the temptation to find a position before leaving the wool business. I made the decision to leave, and then called on some local bank executives with whom I had worked and presented my situation to them. I entered the office of one banking friend in a new relationship. I was no longer the good customer, but was now asking for information concerning future employment. It is amazing how quickly confidence can give way to panic. I knew the wool business. I had the years of experience and skills required in the fibre, trade practices, needs of customers, characteristics of wool from various countries and provinces, and was posted on range conditions. I knew something about international currencies and shipping. How could any of these skills be transferred into another business?

My friend, and bankers can be friends, told me of various corporations looking for chief executive officers and ones in which he thought I could be of help. I was astounded. In my experience I had seen the technical side of a specialty business and didn't, at the time, realize that management is getting things done through people and that the life experience of managing is always needed. The technical aspects of most operations can be learned in a relatively short time. I naturally leaned toward finance and commodities, as this seemed to fit my experience best.

While on a trip to see a customer in the Chicago area I attended a dinner at Wheaton College. Among other friends I met Ken and Jean Hansen. After dinner Ken asked me about business. I briefly told him about my leaving the business and the reasons for doing so. He asked questions concerning the industry that indicated real interest. Most people are really not interested in another's problems. Ken seemed both intellectually curious and personally concerned. He said, "Will you be in Monday morning?" I nodded. "I'll call you." When Ken called he stated that he'd like to visit me in Boston the following week as he had something he felt I should know about.

His conversation when in Boston concerned my going into a joint venture with his company to set up in the Northeast a new operation that would handle housekeeping for hospitals. He extracted a promise and date to spend two days at his operation in Downers Grove, Illinois. I guess I went because I didn't want to hurt his feelings and because I had told the Lord I'd be available for his leading. I had no idea that cleaning hospitals was anything I would want.

After seeing Ken's operation and looking over their figures I was to meet with Ken Hansen, Ken Wessner, and Marion Wade to give my decision. It would be a polite "no." At this time Ken Hansen was President of Wade, Wenger ServiceMaster Inc., Ken Wessner was Vice President, and Marion Wade was Chairman of the Board. I told the triumvirate that while I thought the project had real opportunity, I did not feel this was my area of experience. Mr. Wade seemed surprised and suggested we pray about it. He led in a beautiful prayer, and then Ken Hansen prayed.

While Ken was praying I saw myself as unwilling to accept this kind of work in spite of having told the Lord I'd go where he led. For the first time in my life I saw myself as a stuffed shirt. I was under conviction. Ken Wessner then prayed, and I followed. When I finished, I said I'd take the job and set up a joint-risk operation. When I said this I did what I had never done publicly as an adult—I wept. I was embarrassed and disbelieved my reaction. But I had peace, utter peace. I didn't know what lay ahead, but I knew I had done the right thing. That evening I took our sons to dinner; they were attending Wheaton College. I told them of my decision. Allan replied with a shattering statement, "I don't know why you'd take that job when you'd make a great short-order cook."

I wound up the wool business quickly, and after a short vacation trip to Bermuda I reported for duty at Downers Grove. I was introduced to the department heads and then bought three sets of green work uniforms. At dinner that night Jean Hansen said, "We'll be praying for you as you go through your training experience." She was serious and shortly I was to understand why.

My first assignment was to work for two weeks as a house-man at a large metropolitan hospital. I was to mop corridors, empty trash containers, and clean ash trays. While not in the best condition for this work, I completed the day's schedule. The shock was not in the work but in the general rejection of me as a person because of my green uniform and the kind of work I was doing. Not a single person responded to my "Good Morning" except others in the Housekeeping Department. I had never before experienced the caste system. I had accepted as a seaman the Service code that "Rank Hath Its Privilege."

As the days passed by, I learned a great deal about myself and the needs of people to be accepted. My work strung out into months of being a housekeeping aid, trash collector, linen distributor, linen sorter, floor refinisher, wall washer, and "unit check-out girl." During this period I made some wonderful friends. I began to understand Ken's question to me earlier, "Allan, you are forty-five. You have time for one more career. Are you going to invest your life in things, commodities, or people?" I knew now what he had meant. I was to have a ministry in business to people.

From a financial perspective we were budgeted for losses for two and a half years before the break-even point. We hoped thereafter we would be a profit-making operation. The timetable proved accurate. Upon returning to Boston I began recruiting the team to begin our business. My chief consideration in hiring a manager was "How does he or she see people? Are people to be tools, objects to be exploited, or does this man see people as the objects of the love of God and sense his own responsibility to help develop them?" I had enjoyed the wool business—its international flavor and the great people in it—but now I was excited. This was a "people business" and we were in a position to help employees, patients, hospital administration, and staff alike.

I thought back to my questioning of God's wisdom and faithfulness. I saw why it was necessary for my brook to dry up to make me leave its security to begin a new and wonderful ministry.

Why Hast Thou Forsaken Me?

The Robert E. Lee Hotel in Winston-Salem was the hostelry used by wool salesmen calling on carpet and blanket manufacturing mills and other wool accounts in the area of Central North Carolina. Sir John Rufus* and his wife, Lady Rufus, were my guests for a fortnight trip through the South, visiting mills and being entertained at the homes of the mill owners. Sir John was the Chairman of the Board of our principles, Empire Trading, Ltd.*, through whom we bought Australian, New Zealand, and British wools for our clients and ourselves.

This night we made a late arrival at the Robert E. Lee. After dinner Sir John asked Lady Rufus if she would mind if he and I had a walk about the town. After he escorted her to their room, he returned to meet me in the lobby. He looked quite serious and started talking.

"Allan, I should have told you this a long time ago. Do you remember the first time we stopped at this hotel in 1953? Rooms were scarce and we shared a twin-bedded room. That night, before retiring, you popped out a Bible and began reading. I asked if you would read out loud. That was just ten years ago. As we traveled about I asked

---

* Names altered.

that you read to me morning and evening. Since that time I have never missed a day in reading the Scriptures nor in having a time of prayer. I'd like to tell you why that experience here at this hotel that night was so important.

"As you know, I was a Captain in the Coldstream Guard during the War. We fought under Montgomery, and my Company had crossed a great part of Africa from El Alemain to our present position. We were ordered to attack under a heavy artillery barrage. The Germans were tenaciously pounding us with their heavy guns. We progressed with some casualties, advancing further than our artillery expected. We tried to radio our supporting artillery but we could not make contact. Our own guns were decimating us. I had sent two messengers back, but they never made it. I sent a third, but we were still being pounded by our own guns. The night was clear. The stars were bright in spite of the competition of tracers and exploding shells. I had done about all I could for my men. We were trapped between the enemy fire and our own. I was a churchman, but I did not take religion very seriously. At this moment I felt God close and I said, 'Lord, this looks like the end for all of us, but if You stop our guns from killing us, I'll serve You the rest of my life.'

"Instantly the fire from our batteries ceased and when they commenced again, they had raised elevation. Allan, I did not again think of the promise I had made to God until that night ten years ago in this hotel. The sense of horror I felt that night is still real to me. I had been saved, and immediately forgot my promise. These past ten years have been totally diffcrent. My church attendance has changed. My reading has changed. My priorities have changed. I just wanted you to know."

A week later we were traveling north on the Kentucky Turnpike. Conversation with Sir John and Lady Rufus was always stimulating. I do not remember the subject of the discussion, but Sir John stoutly stated, "I have not a single question concerning the Bible." My mind went quickly back to a conversation I'd had with a mill wool buyer a week before leaving for this trip. He had asked a question I couldn't answer so I posed this question to Sir John. "Why did Jesus say on the cross, 'My God, my God, why hast thou forsaken me' when, as the preexistent second member of the Trinity and Creator, he must have known why he was to be forsaken on the cross? He would have had to know that God could not look upon sin and that he was bearing upon himself the sin of the world."

"That is a good question," replied Sir John. "I had not thought of it. I have in my bag a commentary of Canon Green on the Gospel of Matthew. The quotation is from Matthew. I'll look it up tonight."

This question had never been answered to my own satisfaction. I had understood what I could and accepted the truth that man can never wholly know the mind of God. There had been other questions that had been answered after long delays. I must tell you about Mike Slattery* of the International Hosiery Company*, who had asked this question of me a week before. Mike was a man of great integrity, ingenuous, earthy, profane, but never obscene in conversation, exuberant and a little loud. He was an excellent judge of wool and eminently fair. The salesmen sat on a bench directly outside his office as each awaited his turn and, generally, the "Bench" could hear whether a sale had been made before the salesman in Mike's office had appeared. Mike belonged to the church, but he seldom attended beyond Christmas and Easter. Since I did not stock in quantity the quality of wool purchased by Mike, I had limited exposure to him. The day before Good Friday a competitor called and suggested I invite Mike to a Good Friday service at Park Street Church and then the three of us would go to lunch at the Union Club.

To my surprise Mike was unusually excited about our excursion as we walked briskly to the church, where Dr. Harold John Ockenga was the pastor and was preaching at the service. His subject was "The Last Words of Christ on the Cross." The church, though well filled, emptied rap-

---

* Names altered.

idly and we walked up Park Street to the Club. Mike appeared very sober, and after an unusual period of silence he asked the question I presented later to Sir John. I explained to Mike that these words were an exact quotation from Psalm 22:1 which is a messianic psalm and that as Messiah, Christ had to quote it. But Mike replied, "Then why is it in question form in the 22nd Psalm?" After lunch I called Dr. Ockenga and he stated what I had already told Mike. I called Mike and he ended our conversation with, "Allan, when you find the answer, let me know, will you?" I was amazed at the serious concern this question was to Mike. I just would never have realized Mike would be that concerned about a question of Scripture. I assured him I'd let him know, never thinking that I should glean greater truth concerning this question. The next week I had left on this trip into the South.

We spent the night in Ohio and had a very early morning start. Sir John is not a "morning person" nor is Lady Rufus, but they were at the car at six o'clock, ready to go. Sir John appeared in the best of spirits and had no sooner seated himself in the car when he said, "I've got the answer. It satisfies me. I believe it will you. As soon as we get on the thru-way I'll read you what Canon Green says." Frankly, I had little expectation of any new light on the subject.

I knew Sir John to be not easily moved. He had a Master's degree from Oxford and had studied under C. S. Lewis for one class. I might have been more optimistic. Sir John read aloud. I'll repeat it—as well as I can remember after fourteen years:

> Jewish boys and girls had to memorize psalms and passages concerning the Messiah. The women and John at the foot of the cross must have known by heart the 22nd Psalm. Jesus was at his last physical resources as he hung on the cross. These first words of Psalm 22 identified in the memory of the listeners Jesus' death with the description of this psalm and the details would authenticate him as the Messiah. Since Jesus was limited as to what he could say, he simply started these faithful ones on the psalm they knew by heart.
>
> —"All they that see me laugh me to scorn."
> —"They gaped upon me."

—"All my bones are out of joint."
—"My strength is dried up like a potsherd; and my
　　tongue cleaveth to my mouth."
—"They pierced my hands and my feet."
—"They part my garments among them, and cast lots
　　upon my vesture." Etc.

Just as we might encourage those about us, starting with
the first words of the 23rd Psalm, 'The Lord is my shepherd',
and we would continue through the psalm, so those at the
cross would continue through this 22nd Psalm. Then they
would have the answer to the initial question.

—"All the ends of the world shall remember and turn
　　unto the Lord: and all the kindreds of
　　the nations shall worship before him."
—"For the kingdom is the Lord's: and he is the
　　governor among the nations."
—"A seed shall serve him: it shall be accounted to
　　the Lord for a generation."
—"They shall come, and shall declare his righteousness unto
　　a people that shall be born, that *he hath done this.*"

"What do you think, Allan?"
"It's great!" I replied.
On Monday morning I called Mike straightaway. His
secretary told me that he had a salesman with him. I could
hear Mike calling, "Who is it?" He excused himself to the
salesman and came on the phone.
"Mike, I think I have your answer," and I went on to
tell him the source of my answer. After I shared the explanation, there was a silence on the phone. I thought I heard
Mike say, "Thank You, Lord." I knew I must be imagining
it. Then Mike spoke quietly and with a deep sense of awe.
He said, "Allan, I really had to have an answer to my
question. I prayed for an answer and I knew you'd call
me with the explanation. And now God has answered my
prayer,

　　—through an Australian who comes to this country only
　　once in ten years

　　—through an English clergyman long dead, because of an
　　experience a man had in World War II.

The odds are so against this being just a coincidence! I accept this as a direct answer to prayer. That is why I had to thank the Lord just now. This will change a lot of things in my life."

I hung up, marveling myself at a God who is so personally interested in our needs and in those details that change our lives.

> *The Emery family in 1948 at Bonnie Oaks, Fairlee, Virginia.*
> *Front row: Edward C. Emery, Mr. and Mrs. Emery, Sr., Mabel G. Rowbotham*
> *Back row: Virginia E. Fuller, Allan Emery, Jr., Elsie E. Schoenly*

Final Witness—Part Two

Aunt Blanche was not an aunt by blood relationship, but was one of our adopted "aunts." She lived at the Home for the Aged, a name descriptive, but not very chivalrous to say the least. With her was a pleasant-faced, white-haired little woman. Aunt Blanche was obviously trying to get my attention as I left the church with the rest of the immediate family. I broke rank and Aunt Blanche introduced me to her friend. She said, "I was having dinner at the same table with Mrs. _____ this noon and she asked me why I was so happy. I replied that I was going to a funeral this afternoon. She was horrified and told me she was depressed as it was. I told her to come with me and that she'd feel better." I turned to Mrs. _____ and inquired, "Do you feel happier?" She eagerly answered, "Yes, I never knew that a funeral could be a happy time. Your mother must have been a wonderful person."

I thought of the crowd at the service, the cross-section of people, young, old, black, white, Chinese, poor, wealthy, men, women, children, the good ones and the ones who were better because she had believed in them. Yes, it was a happy time. Mother had lived a life to be ready for death, and in death she continued to be a blessing. At the graveside

we stood singing "Amazing Grace." The funeral directors
looked a little embarrassed. There was harmony, triumph,
and a total conviction in the truth and reality of the last
verse—

> When we've been there ten thousand years,
> Bright shining as the sun,
> We've no less days to sing thy praise
> Than when we first begun.

I've been asked which of my parents was the greater Christian. I can only reply "both." Mother was less frightening
to people than daddy. People felt instantly accepted by her
and of special worth to her. She was beautiful, with deep-
set eyes, white hair, and a lovely smile. She listened well.
Most of my life she had been deaf, not totally, but she
really suffered from it. It had come as a result of improper
medical treatment in her youth. One day a missionary having
dinner with us asked her how many children she had. As
the conversation subject had been on the view from the
house, mother had thought she asked how many acres were
included on the property. When mother replied, "Twenty-
seven" she knew from the shocked expression on the woman's face that she had answered the wrong question!

Mother had known she had cancer for several years. One
night she started hemorrhaging. Sister Elsie called a local
doctor who came right over. As Dr. Alemian walked into
the room mother said, "I'm terribly sorry to interrupt your
evening and I can't get up, but please help yourself to the
chocolates on my dresser." I had arrived at the house before
Dr. Alemian left and he was coming down the stairs as I
entered the front hall. I introduced myself. His only comment to me was, "I've been practicing medicine all my life
but this is the first time anyone ever apologized for not
being able to serve me chocolates. Your mother is a remarka-
ble woman. She is in a terminal illness, and her concern
was one of hospitality for me, not survival for herself."
He left shaking his head. I understood. Day after day, when
I visited her, she asked about Marian and the children with
no complaint about her pain. She had endured a lot of sick-

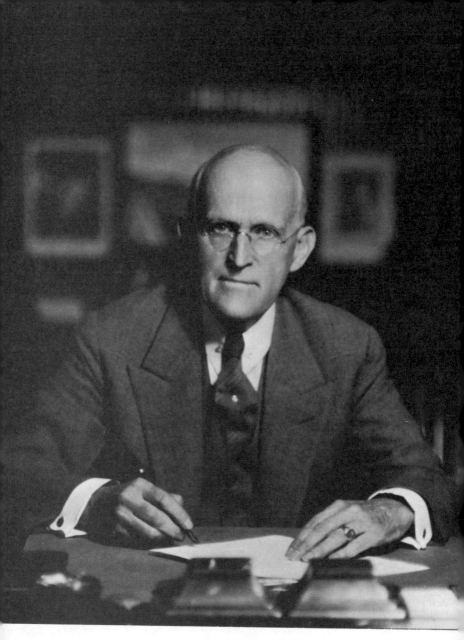

Mr. Allan C. Emery, Sr.

Mr. and Mrs. Allan C. Emery, Sr., on their fiftieth wedding anniversary Oct. 9, 1952, with Grandson, Allan Emery Schoenly

ness during her life and at times, when she suffered most, she could be heard singing,

> Must Jesus bear the cross alone
> And all the world go free?
> No, there's a cross for everyone,
> And there's a cross for me.

Self-pity was unknown to her, and even in the last weeks of her life visitors who came to see her unburdened themselves to her. She remembered birthdays, anniversaries, wrote letters, sent flowers, and listened to everyone's problems. She never talked condescendingly to young people, and "clubbers" would visit her room when she became too weak to sit in her wing chair at Bible Club.

A widow for eleven years, she had carried on amazingly after daddy's death. She told the family her secret. It was shortly after daddy's first stroke and she was optimistic concerning his recovery. I was not. She was always so optimistic. Then, one day I came over and she told me that daddy would not recover but that he would die. I asked her why she had changed her view so suddenly. She said, "Last night I heard a voice, very clear, saying, 'Elsie.' I awakened. I was alone in the room and not at all afraid. The voice said, 'Elsie, I'm going to ask you to trust Me. I am going to take Allan to be with Me.' Instantly I knew it would be all right. I had no fear of losing him. I knew I could trust the One who had spoken. I went back to sleep, but I know he is going to die." The proof of this lay in mother's not shedding a tear at the funeral. She had utter trust in the love of God because of what she had experienced.

Mother memorized Scripture in case she lost her sight. She could recite the verses of most hymns, and she knew poetry by heart. Once she told me that during sleepless nights she had accumulatively recited poetry for seventy-two hours without repeating herself. Mother wrote her diary in French. She could turn a compliment in a way I have never heard equalled.

Mother did not want to die in a hospital. She wanted to be with her loved ones. Elsie, Newt, and their three boys were living at King Oak Hill. We had nurses around the clock. She took no medication, although it was available to her. During her three years with terminal cancer she took one aspirin. Finally she could no longer sit up, and she lay in her bed, the same bed in which I was born. Though in great pain, she always brightened up when one of us came into the room. The nurses were wonderful to her. It was on a Sunday afternoon when she started to sing hymns, "Nearer, Still Nearer," "Must Jesus Bear the Cross Alone?," "Close to Thee," and then "My Jesus I Love Thee." She sang all the verses, but on the last song she sang the verse:

> I'll love thee in life,
> I'll love thee in death,
> And praise Thee as long
> As Thou lendest me breath
> And say when the death dew
> Lies cold on my brow,
> If ever I love Thee
> My Jesus, 'tis now.

Twice she repeated this verse. Then, she turned to Sister Elsie and Gladys and said softly, "I'm going to die now." She slipped into a coma from which she entered the presence of God.

That night I went over to pay the day nurse, who had been there all through mother's final testimony. She said, "I can't take any money for this. It is the greatest spiritual experience I've ever had. It would be a sacrilege."

But, mother's final witness was in the lives of those at the funeral, those at the grave, those to whom she gave herself and before whom she lived as an example of love and purity and faith.

All These Things Are Against Me

"And Jacob their father said unto them, Me have ye bereaved of my children; Joseph is not, and Simeon is not, and ye will take Benjamin away. All these things are against me" (Genesis 42:36).

"And we know that all things work together for good to them that love God, to them who are the called according to his purpose" (Romans 8:28).

The hospital room was quiet as we entered. A young man lay very still but his eyes received us. Obviously he was in great pain and discomfort. There was fear, questioning, courage, and agony written on his face. Ken Hansen and I were visiting Alex Balc at Mount Auburn Hospital in Cambridge. Alex had worked as a ServiceMaster manager before coming East with his family to help me set up our operation in the Northeast. He had been on the operating table for eight and one half hours. At first it appeared that the surgeons would just close up the incision, but the senior surgeon decided to try to perform what might well be a hopeless task. At 6 p.m. the assistant began to close the wound. It had been a close thing, and Alex had a long convalescence to look forward to if all went well. He had thought of how Kathy and the children could get on if he didn't make it. Would his recovery be complete?

We stood at the foot of his bed. Very quietly Ken said, "Alex, you know I have had a number of serious operations. I know the pain of trying to talk. I think I know what questions you are asking. There are two verses I want to give you—Genesis 42:36 and Romans 8:28. We have the option of these two attitudes. We need the perspective of the latter."

He read the verses and then we briefly prayed. With a squeeze of his hand, we left. Our time was up. I'll always remember the strength of Al's parting handclasp.

He had the faith and the will to recover. Today he is Corporate Vice President of ServiceMaster Industries, Inc.

Since that day five years ago I have often thought of those verses and expanded on them. So much of life involves our attitudes to problems. We can see them as road blocks or stepping stones, set-backs or opportunities.

Jacob had good reason to feel that things were against him. He had lost his favorite son Joseph, Rachel's first-born. There was the awful famine that necessitated sending his sons into Egypt to buy grain. Only Benjamin had stayed at home. Now, as the caravan returned, one lad was absent, Simeon, who had remained as hostage until the missing brother Benjamin could go to Egypt and prove to the rough-spoken ruler that the sons of Jacob were not spies. Jacob did not have the benefit we have today of seeing that all the problems had to occur in order for God's covenant promise to the patriarchs to be fulfilled. If Joseph had not been sold by his brothers into Egypt he could not have become ruler under Pharaoh. Without the famine there would have been no need to go to Egypt. We can view the great reunion that Joseph had with his brothers when he revealed himself to them, but Jacob saw only the problems.

The apostle Paul had quite another attitude. Toward the end of his third missionary journey he was constrained to return quickly to Jerusalem as he knew his ministry was there, even though "bonds and afflictions" lay ahead. The apostle called the elders of the church of Ephesus to the little port of Miletus to meet him. He had invested three years in Ephesus and now he said farewell to these leaders whom he loved and to whom he now entrusted the work of this ministry. As he views the problems ahead he says, "But none of these *things* move me, neither count I my life dear unto myself, so that I might finish my course with joy, and the ministry, which I have received of the Lord Jesus, to testify the gospel of the grace of God" (Acts 20:24). What an attitude! Consistent with this attitude, he gives us in Philippians 1:12–14, "But I would ye should understand, brethren, that the *things* which happened unto me have fallen out rather unto the furtherance of the gospel; So that my bonds in Christ are manifest in all the palace, and in all other places; And many of the brethren in the Lord, waxing confident by my bonds, are much more bold to speak the word without fear." Paul was in the palace prison. His fellow-believers and supporters in Philippi must have questioned God's wisdom in letting Paul lie in prison. He assures his friends that the prison is his pulpit, that his guards are a captive audience, and, after hearing the good news from his lips, leave to the far-flung garrisons of the Roman Empire. All the palace knew the message he had from God.

In Romans 8:28 we read, "And we know that all *things* work together for good to them that love God, to them who are the called according to his purpose." In the following verse that purpose is given, "to be conformed to the image of his Son." What is our attitude toward "things"? Are they overwhelming? Are we afraid? Do we blame God? Or do we let him give us perspective to see the ultimate triumph of every life that belongs to him?

My father retained a highly respected lawyer in Boston to handle his estate planning. After the war, I was back in business and daddy had me become familiar with his will and the plans he had made to give mother adequate income at his death. As I learned about estate taxes, I became alarmed that gifts he had made years earlier and on which he had paid gift taxes would be included in his estate as well as in mother's, as powers of appointment had not been released within the time limit specified by law. He couldn't believe this, and we had a meeting at the Parker House with an estate tax expert. Not only were my fears justified, but things were worse than I had expected. At that point, it appeared that it would take more than all the family assets to pay the estate taxes at daddy's death.

We rode in silence from the hotel to the office, and then daddy smiled and said, " 'Naked came I out of my mother's womb, and naked shall I return thither; the Lord gave, and the Lord hath taken away; blessed be the name of the Lord' (Job 1:21). Allan, the Lord has never failed me. I don't know what can be done, but I have every confidence that this experience will be used for his glory and for our good." I doubt if I was ever so proud of daddy as I was then. He appeared a giant casting a shadow over the problem, and his total confidence that God was in control invaded me too. Things did work out. It took time, but through this I learned to trust a God who makes no mistakes. Not a sparrow falls without his knowledge, love, and will.

The Land of Beginning Again

"If we confess our sins, he is faithful and just to forgive us our sins, and to cleanse us from all unrighteousness" (1 John 1:9).

It is pleasant to remember those who in spite of fleeing to a "far country" have made their reconciliation to the Father through the Son.

I was to speak at Summer Bible Club. It was 5 a.m. when the alarm went off at our home in Braintree. I was alone, for Marian and the children were at the farm. Since there would be no time when I arrived at home, I had to prepare a talk before leaving on the road. I sat in the kitchen reading over the lives of biblical characters who had messed up their lives and had, by the grace of God, made a comeback. I was surprised to find so many. Then I thought of those from secular history and made up my outline.

My text was 1 Corinthians 6:11, "And such were some of you: but ye are washed, but ye are sanctified, but ye are justified in the name of the Lord Jesus, and by the Spirit of our God." The list of offenders in the preceding verses seemed to cover everyone, "unrighteous, fornicators, idolaters, adulterers, thieves, covetous, effeminate, abusers of themselves with mankind, drunkards, revilers and extortioners." If there was hope for these, there could be hope for anyone.

The reason for this subject was that one of our old clubbers was back from overseas where he had "freed himself from the old-fashioned ideas of parents and church." From his last letter I sensed a deep yearning for a personal relationship with the Lord Jesus. I wanted him to know he was not alone in having to come back to the Father's house and that every prodigal who repented—turned back—would be accepted. I often speak for a particular one whom I know has a need, and I find that the message has meaning for others as well.

My outline completed, I drove off to my first call two-and-a-half hours away. The mill owner was, as is often the case, the wool buyer. I had an appointment and was shown into his office. My customer was standing behind his desk, looking exhausted and dispirited. He commenced, "The only reason I'm here this morning is because I have an appointment with you. Last night I burned out the engine of my car on the Turnpike and was caught by the trooper who was chasing me. He booked me for going 120 miles an hour and 'being under the influence.' I guess I'll lose my license, but that is just one of my problems." He went on to enumerate his personal problems which started with alcoholism and stretched out to cover family, friends, community, and business. He ended, "So you see I have nothing to live for. After you leave I'm going to end my problems with a bullet. If you know why I shouldn't kill myself, tell me. I'll give you an hour."

It is amazing how quickly priorities can change. I had come expecting to show wool samples and to sell some lots. Wool did not enter either of our minds. I thought of the talk I had prepared that morning and said, "You know, you are not the first person to mess up his life nor will you be the last. I'm speaking to my young people tonight and I'd be happy to tell you what I intend to tell them." I quietly prayed as I spoke, "Lord, this is totally beyond me. I've never spoken to a man about to kill himself. You'll have to take over. Let me be available to You."

As I spoke my friend paced the large area of his office behind his desk. His face was puffed and red. He would shake, tear papers from his desk, crumple them up, and shoot them into his wastepaper basket. I felt a great freedom of being utterly helpless and knowing that God was using my inadequacy in his power. The hour was up, and the case for "The Land of Beginning Again" had been presented and heard. The pacing stopped. He looked at his watch. "We're going out and you are staying with me today." We left in my car, stopping at a garage where my friend purchased a new car as casually as I would buy a book. At lunch he ordered two double drinks of some sort. The first one he was unable to lift to his lips. He steadied down a little and watched me eat my lunch, but he didn't touch his sliced chicken sandwich. Late that afternoon we parted. I had extracted the promise that he would call me before he did anything desperate and that he'd call me early the next morning. He did call and he began the conversation with, "You saved a life but you didn't save a soul."

Last month I had dinner with my friend and his wife. Things have changed over the twenty-three years since that conversation. These have been better and happier years. There are still some problems, and the surrender to the control of the Lord Jesus is still to be made, but the Lord is very patient.

As for Club, the lad for whom I had prepared the talk has never returned home to the Father, but others there that night did. I received a beautiful letter from one prodigal last week. He wrote, "I have for many years viewed myself as a prodigal. When I came back, I tried to return as a hired servant but my Jesus told me I had to come back as a son." As we read the letter Marian and I rejoiced in this great news and in a God who forgives, forgets, and accepts. Luke 15:24 says, "For this my son was dead, and is alive again; he was lost, and is found."

Views of King Oak Hill, the Emery family home

Views of the living room where the Bible club meets

Photos by Richard Matthews

From back first row: Annetta Emery Thurber, whose sketches illustrate this book, and Arthur Hanock Emery. Second row: Richard Judson Thurber, Karen Fontaine Emery, Lynnea Ericksen Emery, and Allan Comstock Emery III. Third row: Joel Allan Emery and Judd Ethan Emery. Fourth row: Allan Comstock Emery, Jr. and Marian Hancock Emery. Fifth row: Todd Chapin Emery and Carolyn Marie Emery.